PRAYING FROM THE
HEAVENLY REALMS

PRAYING FROM THE

HEAVENLY REALMS

SUPERNATURAL SECRETS TO A LIFESTYLE OF ANSWERED PRAYER

KEVIN L. ZADAI

I dedicate this to the Lord Jesus Christ. When I died during surgery and met with Jesus on the other side, He insisted I return to life on the earth and that I help people with their destinies. Because of Jesus's love and concern for people, He would actually send someone back to let them know that their destiny and purpose is secure in Him. I want You to know, Lord, that when You come to take me to be with You someday, I hope that people remember the revelation of Jesus Christ and not me. I am merely being obedient to the heavenly calling and mission You assigned me, Lord Jesus.

ACKNOWLEDGMENTS

In addition to sharing my story with everyone through the books *Heavenly Visitation: A Guide to the Supernatural, Days of Heaven on Earth: A Guide to the Days Ahead, A Meeting Place with God,* and *Your Hidden Destiny Revealed,* the Lord gave me a commission to produce this book, *Praying from the Heavenly Realms: Supernatural Secrets to a Lifestyle of Answered Prayer.* This book addresses some of the revelations concerning the areas that Jesus reviewed and revealed to me, through the Word of God and by the Spirit of God, during several visitations. I want to thank everyone who has encouraged me, assisted me, and prayed for me during the writing of this work, especially my spiritual parents, Dr. Jesse Duplantis and Dr. Cathy Duplantis. Special thanks to my wonderful wife Kathi for her love and dedication to the Lord and to me. Thank you, Sid Roth and staff, for your love of our supernatural Messiah, Jesus. Thank you, Dr. Janet Kline, for the wonderful job editing this book. Thank you, Destiny Image and staff for your support of this project. Special thanks, as well, to all my friends who know about living in two worlds and encountering answered prayer through heavenly visitation!

DESTINY IMAGE® PUBLISHERS, INC.

P.O. Box 310, Shippensburg, PA 17257-0310

"Promoting Inspired Lives."

This book and all other Destiny Image and Destiny Image Fiction books are available at Christian bookstores and distributors worldwide.

Cover design by Eileen Rockwell

Interior design by Terry Clifton

For more information on foreign distributors, call 717-532-3040.

Reach us on the Internet: www.destinyimage.com.

ISBN 13 TP: 978-0-7684-1812-5
ISBN 13 eBook: 978-0-7684-1813-2
ISBN 13 HC: 978-0-7684-1815-6
ISBN 13 LP: 978-0-7684-1814-9

For Worldwide Distribution, Printed in the U.S.A.

2 3 4 5 6 7 8 / 22 21 20 19 18

CONTENTS

FOREWORD

I am so blessed to introduce you to Kevin Zadai and his wonderful book, *Praying from the Heavenly Realms*. Kevin is not only a friend, but he is also one of my spiritual sons, and it's such a blessing to see what God is doing in his life and growing ministry. Get ready to be blessed!

Kevin has a great revelation of what God is doing, what God has done, and what God will do. How do I know that? Well, you see, Kevin died and had a visitation from Jesus. And buddy, let me tell you, when you meet Jesus you come away with greater knowledge, insight, and understanding—and you've also got something to say! In this book, Kevin's got something to say that will totally revolutionize the way you see God and how you pray (or talk) to Him.

God desires to fellowship with us and has so much in store for us if we would simply just plug in to Him. You will learn that "Fellowship is communication, dialogue, and sharing intimate secrets. It should not be done because it's required, but because it is your passion. The Lord wants to have fellowship with you. …It is His passion." I love that— passion. God is passionate about *you*—think about that! As you read this book, you will come away with a greater passion for God and a greater desire to talk with Him than ever before. It will bring you to another level in your relationship with Him. That's what this book is all about. I encourage you to read it and learn how to pray from the heavenly realms with ease.

JESSE DUPLANTIS
Author, Speaker, TV Host
President and Founder of Jesse Duplantis Ministries

INTRODUCTION

Theoretically, when we read the Scriptures it is clear that true believers live in two worlds simultaneously. But practically, how do we do this?

It took a man who had an experience like the apostle Paul—when he was caught up to the third heaven—to bring back this revelation.

Kevin Zadai was a "normal" Christian until he left his body during a dental procedure and found himself in Heaven. He pleaded with Jesus to *not* send him back, but Jesus explained that Kevin was not coming back for himself but for others.

I believe Kevin came back for every reader of this book. We are in the last of the last days, and believers must get all their prayers answered. Until now, only a handful in every generation would see their prayers quickly answered. This next move of God's Spirit must have believers able to pray from the heavenly realms. This means that believers will step into a new "normal"—only this normal will be defined by the Bible.

The Bible makes it clear that even though we live on earth, we are also seated with Messiah Jesus in the heavenly realms (see Eph. 2:6 NIV). This place of supernatural access is also a place of intimacy. This intimacy is your inheritance in Messiah Jesus. You can enjoy the supernatural fellowship with God that Jesus told us about. He said, "I no longer call you slaves, because a master doesn't confide in his slaves. Now you are my friends, since I have told you everything the Father told me" (John 15:15 NLT).

I don't see Kevin Zadai as some extraordinary or unusual case; he is an example of the level of intimacy and friendship God is calling all believers into. Every reader of this book has access to this! And when the Master confides in you, like the Scripture says, you hear God's words with clarity and you are able to *pray His words*. When you pray the words that God is speaking, you are praying from the heavenly realms and *these prayers* will receive answers. You *will* receive your breakthrough when your prayers are birthed in that realm!

And when you have your breakthrough, you will be prepared to equip the millions of new believers that are about to come to the Lord to get their prayers answered.

When you learn how to pray from the heavenly realms, your intimacy and fellowship with God will exponentially increase. Out of this new-found intimacy you will fulfill your full destiny.

Shalom and love,
SID ROTH
Host, *It's Supernatural!*

Chapter 1

GETTING HEAVEN'S ATTENTION

*Jesus wants everyone to yield to the Holy Spirit and
participate in the supernatural every day!*

"You met Jesus face to face?!" people ask.

"Yes!" I respond with excitement. Then, people usually want to know what Jesus looks like. It is the number-one question I get asked the instant people find out about my encounter with Him during my *heavenly visitation*. Well, His description is beyond words! I will at least try to describe Him. But first, let me tell you how it all started.

In 1992, I was scheduled to go in for a day surgery to remove my impacted wisdom teeth. In a prep room, I was sedated and told to count down from one hundred. I didn't get very far before I became unconscious. Then, I was suddenly outside my body and standing beside the operating table, watching the surgeon and his two assistants work.

When I realized that I had passed on, I wanted to inform the doctor. It was to no avail. I could no longer communicate with the earthly realm. As I waited there in the operating room, I witnessed my body on the table begin to glow with a glistening white light, and suddenly my body was transformed into what looked like perfection to me. I resembled an angel. My face looked like mine but was so bright and perfect. I thought, *I look beautiful.* That was when I heard a man's voice behind me say, "That's what you look like to Me all the time!" I turned around, and that was when I saw Him.

Jesus was the most handsome King I had ever laid eyes on. He had a beautiful, full-length robe on and was about five feet ten inches tall. He had long hair that looked like a lion's mane. His eyes were so deep and full of destiny. His presence demanded my attention as I stood there in adoration.

However, what Jesus looked like was not the most impactful thing about Him. I always steer people toward what *He said to me!* Are you ready to hear what Jesus taught me? He began to teach me how the supernatural realm works. First, He taught me that *words* were of utmost importance to the operation of the realm of the supernatural. Jesus began to teach me with conviction about the use of my words. He explained how the supernatural realm responds to me when I speak by the Holy Spirit with an *authority and faith* born from the *Spirit's revelation*, not my own understanding, producing what is called a *faith rest.*

The end result was that I could have what I said by the Holy Spirit, and this would always bring about my destiny. He taught me that I could have the perfect will of God all the time and that I should speak to my mountains without hesitation (see Mark 11:23-24). He even showed me that each one of my days was written in a book before one of them came to pass (Ps. 139:16). This was the main desire of the Holy Spirit—to pray out and accomplish my destiny from my written book in Heaven every day. He also reminded me that I would give an account for every idle word that came out of my mouth (see Matt. 12:36).

Second, Jesus taught me that the *single most important thing* that I could do to participate in the supernatural realm was to pray in tongues. This practice will take the limitations off your life as the Spirit brings liberty to any situation. You are praying out the mysteries of God when you yield to Him. The Holy Spirit reveals God's heart to you (see 1 Cor. 2:9-15). You can increase this kind of praying without limit (see 1 Cor. 14:18). I was told that praying in tongues would lead me into situations where I would increase financially instead of decreasing; I would have appointments and not disappointments because there are no disappointments in Heaven. Jesus said that the Holy Spirit doesn't know defeat, and I should yield to Him continually.

During this *heavenly visitation,* He took me to the White Sands Missile Range in New Mexico and showed me how powerful my prayers were. As I prayed "in the Spirit" at His command, what looked like an atomic blast in the desert erupted. It sent a billowing fire upward. Jesus pointed out that it was not the "spectacular" mushroom cloud that made prayer effective when people pray, but the shockwave that moved along the ground that was causing everything to be moved out of the way. He told me that the shockwave was the supernatural, not the spectacular mushroom cloud that rose skyward. He let me know that the shockwaves were the effects of my supernatural prayers. He encouraged me to always believe that my prayers were effective and to never give up.

Third, Jesus explained to me that the time is short and that I should yield to the Holy Spirit's work in my life. We must allow the acceleration of the Holy Spirit's training as a very important aspect to the operation in the supernatural realm. He explained that He used to have years and years to train people for what He had assigned for them to do. He used Moses as an example—he had 40 years training in Pharaoh's court and then 40 years in the Midian desert as a shepherd. Jesus said that now it is days of training instead of the years that were available previously. He encouraged me to allow the acceleration of the Spirit's training to be completed without hindrance on my part.

Jesus wanted me to know that everything I do in faith counts and is rewarded. He also told me that if I did something for someone in His name, I would be rewarded for it, even if it were just a cup of water. Everything is recorded and it is all rewarded! There is no loss in Him as we allow the ministry of Jesus to come forth.

To operate in the supernatural realm in the coming years, we must allow the Holy Spirit to do these three things in our midst. First, we must allow the Holy Spirit to reveal Jesus to us! He is the Way, the Truth, and the Life. The apostle Paul prayed for the Ephesians that the eyes of their hearts would be enlightened (see Eph. 1:17-23). He prayed that a Spirit of wisdom and *revelation* would be on them.

Second, Jesus wants to visit us by His Spirit in a greater manner. It's time for the next wave of visitation, and it will come after the revelation of Jesus comes forth through the Word and the Spirit coming together. Visitation needs to come forth in a stronger way.

And third, the result of *revelation* and *visitation* is *habitation*. This is where the Father and Jesus come to visit and decide to stay and make their abode with us (John 14:23). Then the glory rests! We are living in the most exciting times. The final harvest is coming in!

Drinking the New Wine

In this chapter, we will look at all the characteristics of a believer who is yielding to the Holy Spirit for the preparation of the wedding day with Jesus Christ. We will also investigate the influence and effective harvest made possible to those who will participate in the arrival of the "deluge of the Spirit," which is the great outpouring of the Spirit. As Jesus's first miracle, which was the miracle of water into wine, becomes His last miracle through the Church, we see the water of the Word become the new wine of the Spirit. That new wine brings such awesome Holy Spirit encounters to the people of the earth. This first chapter will ultimately produce a successful prayer life by itself, which includes *heavenly visitation* during prayer. The Spirit can make you a person to whom others are drawn supernaturally by pouring out His Spirit on you. The "new wine" of the Spirit can be *overwhelming* as Jesus invades your world by His Spirit.

> *This is how God makes you someone who draws others into a fuller relationship with Him that is supernatural. When His realm hits your realm and you get overwhelmed, I call it being "OverRealmed!"*

Others mocking said, "They are full of new wine." But Peter, standing up with the eleven, raised his voice and said to them, "Men of Judea and all who dwell in Jerusalem, let this be known to you, and heed my words. For these are not drunk, as you suppose, since it is only the third hour of the day. But this is what was spoken by the prophet Joel: 'And it shall come to pass in the last days, says God, that I will pour out of My Spirit on all flesh; your sons and your daughters shall prophesy, your young men shall see visions, your old men shall dream dreams. And on My menservants and on My maidservants, I will pour out My Spirit in those days; and they shall prophesy. I will show wonders in heaven above and signs in the earth beneath: blood and fire and vapor of smoke. The sun shall be turned into darkness, and the moon into blood, before the coming of the great and awesome day of the Lord. And it shall come to pass that whoever calls on the name of the Lord shall be saved'" (Acts 2:13-21).

God's next outpouring is here! The Holy Spirit and the heavenly hosts are ready for the harvest. The Holy Spirit, at the same time, is building up the body of Christ and preparing the bride of Christ for the wedding feast. "For these are not drunk, as you suppose, since it is only the third hour of the day."

> *Let the Presence of God help you get over yourself. It is not about you!*

Know His Thoughts Toward You

When Jesus was standing with me after I had died in the operating room during my *heavenly visitation* in 1992, I remember looking into His eyes and seeing something amazing. He remembered the day He thought of me and spoke me into existence and sent me to my mother's womb. This is extremely important to understand because I could hear Jesus's thoughts when I looked into His eyes. When He realized this He smiled. He saw that I had turned out just as He desired when He spoke me into existence. I had turned out the perfect way that He intended me to be. It is profound how much He loves people. God's purpose is actually injected into us when we are created, along with the gifts and plans that He has for us. His purpose for His Kingdom has been placed inside of you, and this earthly life is just a journey of discovery. There is an unfolding of the gifts of God and the purpose of God for every person on the earth. He does not wish that any should perish. The Spirit spoke through the prophet Jeremiah, saying:

For I know the thoughts that I think toward you, says the Lord, thoughts of peace and not of evil, to give you a future and a hope. Then you will call upon Me and go and pray to Me, and I will listen to you. And you will seek Me and find Me, when you search for Me with all your heart (Jeremiah 29:11-13).

Accountability

The very spot in front of the throne from which my spirit was created is where I will return to give an account for what I did with what I was given in the flesh. I will lay it all down before Him in the very spot I was created. It was a circular pattern. His Word went out and came back and produced a harvest; it did not come back void.

This is very important, because in this way God revealed He was the author and finisher of my faith. So I was given a seed of faith at my new creation, and He is the finisher of my faith before whom I will stand at the end of my life with the harvest because He is the Alpha and the Omega, the Beginning and the End.

Your Destiny Package

God has a Father's heart. When He recreated the human spirit of each individual who has been born again, He placed within him or her a package that contains his or her destiny. These packages need to be unwrapped, explored, and discovered. Gifts of wisdom and knowledge have been placed within those packages. Everyone is special and very essential to this earth because of those gifts that they have been assigned by God before birth to be activated as they enter into a new, born-again life. We depend upon each other. The apostle Paul explained that this is God's desire for us:

But, speaking the truth in love, may grow up in all things into Him who is the head—Christ—from whom the whole body, joined and knit together by what every joint supplies, according to the effective working by which every part does its share, causes growth of the body for the edifying of itself in love (Ephesians 4:15-16).

It is important to understand that we need to find salvation through Jesus Christ and become born again. Our new birth in Him activates our spirit and the gifts that are within us. The Holy Spirit brings forth our destiny as we start participating in our part of God's Kingdom. Everything that is innocent and everything that we do with what is in us counts and we receive rewards. We need each other.

> *The Lord knows when you sacrifice. He asks, "What have you done?" This is so special, and He rewards you.*

Everything Counts

Every person counts, and everything you do with what God has given you counts. You are greatly rewarded for what you do in faith. Hebrews 11:6 was completely explained to me. When I was with Jesus, after I had died on the operating table, one of the lessons I learned from Him was that everything I do for Him counts. I was taught that if I did something in faith, it was recorded and I was rewarded for that act of faith. Also, Jesus told me that even if I did something in His name, I was rewarded simply because I wanted to represent Him in an honorable way.

Without faith, you cannot please God. I realize that it is not just enough to believe that God exists, but we must also believe that He a Rewarder of those who *diligently* seek Him. Jesus *has so much love for everyone*, but He needs for you to yield to the Holy Spirit and His faithful angels. They have been sent to expedite your destiny. He wants you to *tell* Him how much you trust Him every day. He wants you to *show* Him how much you trust Him every day in your actions.

Immediate Obedience

Jesus told me during my *heavenly visitation* in 1992 that I had been faithful in all that He had ever asked me to do for Him. He mentioned that I am known in Heaven. He explained that Heaven speaks of me because of a character trait that is uncommon on the earth. He said that it is rare to find someone such as I, who will always drop what I am doing and immediately do whatever the Spirit is doing at the time. He said, "And you never even ask Me for an explanation; you just do it."

> *We are not to take advantage of our position in Christ by living a lukewarm life. Our relationship with Him should reflect the position we have been given by the sacrifice of Jesus.*

Relational Holiness and Righteousness

Once, I was taken to the throne room and stood before a large sapphire stone floor that was burning white hot with blue. It looked like it was alive. It was very holy. The Lord told me that I could not walk on this pavement unless He bid me to come, that it was for those who had chosen to walk before Him in holiness. To walk in that place, one must stay separate from the world. He explained to me that there is a positional holiness and a positional righteousness. Also, there is relational holiness and relational righteousness. I was told that many believers want to live their lives on the outskirts where the fences are found. They attempt to get as far in the world as they can without losing their salvation. They try to live in both the world and in God. He explained to me that we are supposed to go where the fire of holiness and righteousness can be found. We are to position ourselves as close as possible to the fire of holiness and righteousness. He said that this place was where the *relational holiness* and righteousness are found. He said that going to the outskirts closer to the fence was depending upon someone's positional stand. He explained that by the blood of Jesus, we are given a special position in holiness and righteousness. *We are not to take advantage of our position in Christ by living a lukewarm life.* Our relationship with Him should reflect the position we have been given by the sacrifice of Jesus.

Chapter 2

WHY AREN'T MY PRAYERS
BEING ANSWERED?

Becoming Good Soil

When we reveal, implement, and practice our covenant with the
Lord Jesus Christ in our lives, then we become attractive to Heaven.
If Heaven is for you, then you must accept this as a fact. We must be
people who are led by the Spirit of God so that we are actually able
to have the Kingdom of God begin to work in our lives. If only we
would allow the Holy Spirit to communicate this to us, we would do
so much better.

On one occasion, Jesus spoke with me about the parable of the
sower. I was shocked at how much I did not understand about this parable. After seeking God, I realized that this parable is concentrating on
the condition of the soil and should be referred as the *parable of the soil*
instead. Let us look deeply into what Jesus taught in this parable. But

before we do this, I would like to quote what Jesus said about this parable from the Aramaic language, which He spoke fluently:

> *"If you're able to understand this, then you need to respond."*
> *Then his disciples approached Jesus and asked, "Why do*
> *you always speak to people in these hard-to-understand*
> *parables?" He explained, "**You've been given the inti-***
> ***mate experience of insight into the hidden truths and***
> ***mysteries of the reign of heaven's kingdom**, but they*
> *have not. For everyone who listens with an open heart will*
> *receive progressively more revelation until he has more than*
> *enough. But those who don't listen with an open, teachable*
> *heart, even the understanding that they think they have will*
> *be taken from them"* (Matthew 13:9-12 TPT).

Wow! I can just hear Jesus saying this and letting us know that He wants us to meditate on His words until those words become so much a part of us that what He says influences every aspect of our lives. "You've been given the *intimate experience of insight* into the *hidden truths* and *mysteries* of the *reign of heaven's kingdom!*" The Spirit of God seeks out the deep things of God. "But God has revealed them to us through His Spirit. For the Spirit searches all things, yes, the deep things of God" (1 Cor. 2:10).

I want to know the deep things of God. Jesus said that if we understand the parable of the sower, we have been given the deep, intimate, hidden truths and mysteries of the Kingdom of Heaven. Because we understand that God offers us such great understanding of His truths, we must respond. I have to share these truths with you because you are going to be effective in prayer and get every prayer answered when you fully understand what I am explaining.

> *Then He spoke many things to them in parables, saying:*
> *"Behold, a sower went out to sow. And as he sowed, some*

seed fell by the wayside; and the birds came and devoured them. Some fell on stony places, where they did not have much earth; and they immediately sprang up because they had no depth of earth. But when the sun was up they were scorched, and because they had no root they withered away. And some fell among thorns, and the thorns sprang up and choked them. But others fell on good ground and yielded a crop: some a hundredfold, some sixty, some thirty. He who has ears to hear, let him hear!"

And the disciples came and said to Him, "Why do You speak to them in parables?"

He answered and said to them, "Because it has been given to you to know the mysteries of the kingdom of heaven, but to them it has not been given. For whoever has, to him more will be given, and he will have abundance; but whoever does not have, even what he has will be taken away from him. Therefore I speak to them in parables, because seeing they do not see, and hearing they do not hear, nor do they understand. And in them the prophecy of Isaiah is fulfilled, which says: 'Hearing you will hear and shall not understand, and seeing you will see and not perceive; for the hearts of this people have grown dull. Their ears are hard of hearing, and their eyes they have closed, lest they should see with their eyes and hear with their ears, lest they should understand with their hearts and turn, so that I should heal them'" (Matthew 13:3-15).

Here is where we must receive the Spirit of revelation that Paul talked about in the book of Ephesians:

That the God of our Lord Jesus Christ, the Father of glory, may give to you the spirit of wisdom and revelation in the knowledge of Him, the eyes of your understanding being enlightened (Ephesians 1:17-18).

Listen as Jesus explains these truths to us. Remember that we must have "eyes that see and ears that hear."

> *But blessed are your eyes, because they see; and your ears, because they hear. I tell you the truth, many prophets and righteous people longed to see what you see, but they didn't see it. And they longed to hear what you hear, but they didn't hear it.*
>
> *Now listen to the explanation of the parable about the farmer planting seeds: The seed that fell on the footpath represents those who hear the message about the Kingdom and don't understand it. Then the evil one comes and snatches away the seed that was planted in their hearts. The seed on the rocky soil represents those who hear the message and immediately receive it with joy. But since they don't have deep roots, they don't last long. They fall away as soon as they have problems or are persecuted for believing God's word. The seed that fell among the thorns represents those who hear God's word, but all too quickly the message is crowded out by the worries of this life and the lure of wealth, so no fruit is produced. The seed that fell on good soil represents those who truly hear and understand God's word and produce a harvest of thirty, sixty, or even a hundred times as much as had been planted!* (Matthew 13:16-23 NLT)

The Sower

A farmer plants seeds. *Webster's Dictionary, 1828 Edition* defines a *sower* as "he that scatters seed for propagation. One who scatters or spreads; as a sower of words."

The Seed

The seed is the Word. According to *Webster's, seed* is "the substance, animal or vegetable, which nature prepares for the reproduction and conservation of the species. The seeds of plants are a deciduous part, containing the rudiments of a new vegetable."

The Ground

Finally, Webster defined *ground* as "the surface of land or upper part of the earth, without reference to the materials which compose it."

The Four Types of Soil in Matthew 13

The Footpath:

It is very important to not only hear what God is saying, but understand it as well. Jesus, in person, wanted me to grasp truth being taught. He wanted me to take truth into my heart so that it produced a crop. Remember, it is possible to hear but walk away ***not understanding*** it. Don't let the evil one come and ***snatch away*** the Word that was planted in your heart.

The Rocky Soil:

We all have had the experience of hearing the Word of God and encountering such an awesome joy. We need to make sure that we have a depth concerning our walk with God. Our commitment level will determine our longevity during ***troubles***. When we are ***persecuted*** for believing God's Word, we will not relinquish our joy and produce a crop.

The Thorns:

Many of us are very busy concerning the affairs of this life on earth. We must not allow the Word to be crowded out by the ***worries*** of this life and the ***attraction of wealth***. The thorns are pushing out the truth of the Kingdom in your soil.

The Good Soil:

The good soil is the heart that truly receives and understands what God is saying and produces an amazing harvest, even a hundred times as much as had been planted!

The most interesting characteristic about Jesus is this: He is so simple in His approach toward truth. He gave us a sincere way to understand the way that the Kingdom of Heaven works. It is interesting to note that there is nothing to be done with the seed except to sow it. The farmer sows the seed. That is what farmers do. The Lord Jesus instructed me that the seed has everything within it and is missing nothing essential to growth. A seed contains, within itself, all that is necessary for propagation. Once planted, it sprouts and produces a crop. Keep this in mind—one does not have to do anything else but just plant, water, and wait.

Every time I am speaking at a conference, I begin to minister on certain subjects concerning people's hearts through the word of knowledge. I am really ministering to their soil, which may contain rocks and thorns and other hindrances that prevent the soil's production of the Word that is sown. The Lord showed me when I came back that I should deal with the soil first, getting it ready for the sowing of the Word by ministering to the people through the word of knowledge, word of wisdom, discerning of spirits, and prophecy. He told me that if I would do this, I would see a greater harvest when I did sow the Word during the teaching time.

The teaching time occurs during the service, after this period of time. It may take ten minutes or an hour. To most people, it may seem as if I am randomly talking, but what I am really doing is getting rid of any hindrances in those who are listening so that the Word of God takes root and produces a crop in those individuals. Jesus comes and stands beside me and tells me the people's hearts. Once I know the conditions that exist, I will start to speak out on certain subjects and minister to the people en mass or individually, however God so chooses. After the Lord takes care of the issues with the people's soil, the glory will come in as I minister the Word to the people. He also tells me to speak to the staff of the church or ministry separately in a closed session. He will tell me at times to speak to the intercessory prayer group and the worship group as well in a closed session. He told me that if I could get the leadership on the same page as Him, the rest of the church or ministry would follow.

It Is Not About You

While I was on the other side with Jesus, before I came back to this life, one of the most profound things that I learned was how important it is to understand how this life works after you have given Him your life and allowed the Spirit of God to make your spirit new by the new birth or being "born again." I remember when Jesus smiled at me in the visitation of 1992 when I told Him I was not going back to the earth. I wanted to be with Him in Heaven forever, and I felt so safe and comfortable with Him and all that His presence has to offer. He let me know that I was needed back on the earth for the purpose of helping to fulfill other people's destinies and not just my own. I understand how important it was for me to come back and play out the strategies of Jesus and His Kingdom, strategies that are beyond my own personal world. It was awesome to know how much Jesus truly has planned for each person on the earth. Unfortunately, most people have no idea of the things that He has written and designed for them or that these plans were conceived long before they were born. God planned to send me back to this life because He means to use my life to be a real game-changer for many people who need to hear from Heaven. People's destinies continue to be confirmed as God brings revelation and correction to people to whom

He sends me. He told me, "You will sense Me come and stand beside you and whisper in your right ear what I want you say to the person to whom I have ordained you to speak. They will be rerouted onto the path that was chosen for them and will never be the same again." Because of all that He showed me about His will for people, I must tell you some very important things that I now know.

God's Will

God's will is already established in Heaven. His will includes many different aspects of life. His will is understandably the way of life in Heaven. No one resists it. His Word is no different than who He is as a person. Whatever He says, He will do. His Word is His will. We can learn His will by reading and consuming every word that He has spoken that is recorded. The intent of His Word is just as important as His Word. To comprehend His Word's full intent takes a little more time than just reading and quoting the Word. You must let the Holy Spirit reveal the intent of the word spoken. You must coordinate His word with other scriptures in the Word of God.

There are also books written in Heaven for individuals. These books are His will as well (see Ps. 139:16). Angels work constantly according to the Word and will of God for individuals. This fact is important to know when praying because there is a way to pray that will always get the answer. Remember, He wants to do His will in your life. The Holy Spirit reveals His will in the words that God has spoken.

Faith Rest

We know that without faith, we cannot please God (see Heb. 11:6). There is a resting place in which we must live, and that is the goal of faith. Enter into the "secret place" (see Ps. 91). Until you reach this place of rest, you are still warring against doubt. This warfare against unbelief persists when revelation has not yet come through the Holy Spirit. When a person is in doubt, then faith is not ruling. It is one thing to hear the Word of God; it is quite another to embrace it by experience and find it igniting your inner being. Faith takes the promise and implements it by revelation in the Holy Spirit.

> *Now God has offered to us the same promise of entering into his realm of resting in confident faith. So we must be extremely careful to ensure that we all embrace the fullness of that promise and not fail to experience it. For we have heard the good news of deliverance just as they did, **yet they didn't join their faith with the Word and activate its power.** Instead, what they heard didn't affect them deeply, for they doubted. For those of us who believe, faith activates the promise and we experience the realm of confident rest!* (Hebrews 4:1-3 TPT)

Consider inviting the Holy Spirit to lead you into the revelation of *resting in faith*. He wants to lead you into all truth. He knows nothing else. The Spirit is willing but the flesh is weak (see Matt. 26:41).

Prayer Fruit

We need to get a revelation of what it truly means to be connected to the source of our life. Successful prayer is praying correctly and receiving the answer from God. When you have the Word of God in you, which means that His will is within you and the Spirit of God is your life source, you can ask for anything you want *and it will be done for you!*

> *I am the true grapevine, and my Father is the gardener. He cuts off every branch of mine that doesn't produce fruit,*

and he prunes the branches that do bear fruit so they will produce even more. You have already been pruned and purified by the message I have given you. Remain in me, and I will remain in you. For a branch cannot produce fruit if it is severed from the vine, and you cannot be fruitful unless you remain in me. Yes, I am the vine; you are the branches. Those who remain in me, and I in them, will produce much fruit. For apart from me you can do nothing. Anyone who does not remain in me is thrown away like a useless branch and withers. Such branches are gathered into a pile to be burned. But if you remain in me and my words remain in you, you may ask for anything you want, and it will be granted! When you produce much fruit, you are my true disciples. This brings great glory to my Father (John 15:1-8 NLT).

When we desire to receive answers to prayer, receiving those answers as believers, it depends upon the Lord. We must know what is the will of God. We are able to obtain understanding of His will first by knowing His Word. We can get our needs and desires met when we have a life connection with the vine and when faith is present. Remember that God is greater than any earthly parent (see Matt. 7:7-11; Luke 11:9-13; Rom. 8:32; James 1:5). We need to be taught by the Holy Spirit to experience God as a loving Father who wants to do more for us than we can imagine.

The Father's Willingness

And don't be concerned about what to eat and what to drink. Don't worry about such things. These things dominate the thoughts of unbelievers all over the world, but your Father already knows your needs. Seek the Kingdom of God above all else, and he will give you everything you need. So don't be afraid, little flock. For it gives your Father great happiness to give you the Kingdom (Luke 12:29-32 NLT).

It is wonderful to know that when we concentrate on the powerful Kingdom of God, we will see all of our needs met. When we pray, we find ourselves in a place of provision where we are no longer praying for ourselves but only those things that the Spirit desires. We find that the Spirit will side with us as we focus on the Kingdom and not on selfishness. When we are not selfish, God will start surprising us by giving us the desires of our heart. "Delight yourself also in the Lord, and He shall give you the desires of your heart. Commit your way to the Lord, trust also in Him, and He shall bring it to pass" (Ps. 37:4-5). Also, remember that everyone who asks receives. When you seek, you find, and when you knock on a door, it shall be opened. This is the heavenly Father, who gives you the Holy Spirit when you ask Him. The Holy Spirit will lead you into all truth, which includes anything your heart desires that originates from the Spirit of reality.

> *So I say to you, ask, and it will be given to you; seek, and you will find; knock, and it will be opened to you. For everyone who asks receives, and he who seeks finds, and to him who knocks it will be opened. If a son asks for bread from any father among you, will he give him a stone? Or if he asks for a fish, will he give him a serpent instead of a fish? Or if he asks for an egg, will he offer him a scorpion? If you then, being evil, know how to give good gifts to your children, how much more will your heavenly Father give the Holy Spirit to those who ask Him!* (Luke 11:9-13)

Be confident that not only are your prayers heard but they are also answered when you pray with the assistance of the Holy Spirit. No good thing will He withhold from those who love and walk with Him in the

Spirit of truth (reality). "For the Lord God is a sun and shield; the Lord will give grace and glory; no good thing will He withhold from those who walk uprightly" (Ps. 84:11).

Jesus Is the Commander

Looking away [from all that will distract] to Jesus, Who is the Leader and the Source of our faith [giving the first incentive for our belief] and is also its Finisher [bringing it to maturity and perfection]. He, for the joy [of obtaining the prize] that was set before Him, endured the cross, despising and ignoring the shame, and is now seated at the right hand of the throne of God (Hebrews 12:2 AMPC).

Remember that when you pray, Jesus is the reason that you can pray to the Father and be heard. We pray in Jesus's name because of the *mediation* that Jesus accomplished through His death, burial, and resurrection. He is the author and finisher of our faith. It is because of faith that we see our answers come. Answers do not come forth because of our crying or complaining. "Without faith, it is impossible to please Him" (Heb. 11:6).

When I have met Jesus on numerous occasions, He reveals the personality of a Commander. I had the heavenly impression that if I let Him be in charge of anything in my life, I know I would see the management of that particular aspect of my life and its full completion would come forth. He is in control, and whatever He says goes!

If you need help in any area of your life, ask Him now! Let Jesus be your Commander. He can help you with your prayer life. He lived in a body on the earth just like you. He prayed to the Father for help. "Who, in the days of His flesh, when He had offered up prayers and supplications, with vehement cries and tears to Him who was able to save Him from death, and was heard because of His godly fear" (Heb. 5:7).

Do not ever doubt that Jesus can make a difference when He is allowed to take charge. To trust Him fully and have no doubt that He will answer takes great faith. The centurion in Jesus's day got the highest compliment of anyone concerning his faith. He told Jesus to only speak the word and it shall be done. In the Complete Jewish Bible for this passage in Matthew 8, the phrase *just speak the word* is actually translated *"Only give the command."*

> **Yeshua said, "I will go and heal him."** *But the officer answered, "Sir, I am unfit to have you come into my home. Rather, if you will* **only give the command***, my orderly will recover. For I too am a man under authority. I have soldiers under me, and I say to this one, 'Go!' and he goes; to another, 'Come!' and he comes; to my slave, 'Do this!' and he does it." On hearing this Yeshua was amazed and said to the people following him, "Yes! I tell you, I have not found anyone in Isra'el with such trust!"* (Matthew 8:7-11 CJB).

> *For the Lord, our ruler, the Lord, our commander, the Lord, our king—he will deliver us* (Isaiah 33:22 NET).

Jesus's Character Revealed

Meeting with Jesus has left a great impression upon me concerning His character. His character, as revealed to me, is astonishing. You do not have to do anything but study all the quotes from Him in the Gospels (the red letters) to get a flavor for who He is as a person. He is an exact image of the Father. He only does and says what His Father does and says. When you start to allow the Spirit of God to counsel you, He will tell you the truth about Jesus's character. You will begin to comprehend the ways of God. Most people just know God by His acts. They merely know Him by observing Him; they do not know Him by having a vital relationship with Him. I want to know the intricacies of how God operates. In other words, I want to rule and reign with Him (see 2 Tim. 2:12). Moses knew God's ways. He encountered God on a personal level. "He revealed his character to Moses and his deeds to the people of Israel" (Ps. 103:7 NLT).

Please understand this truth: I have encountered Him several times on a more intimate level, and I have therefore been dramatically changed. A great amount of influence and power flows out from His person. You cannot spend time in His presence without being radically changed. Even His face will cause your face to be changed. When perfection comes in contact with imperfection, something has to give. Jesus is supernatural. When He comes in contact with you, the natural will have to give way to the supernatural.

Many people think they are right about what they believe about Him. However, when you encounter Him in person for the first time, you will realize you are corrected and changed. He is always right about everything. You realize that when you encounter Him. We need to allow Him to influence us in our prayer life. When I met Him, He had such tenacity about Him. His character was to get things accomplished, no matter what the cost. I know now that it would never be wisdom to be a hindrance between the place Jesus stands and the place where He intends to go. Yes, Jesus is compassionate and understanding. He is touched with the feelings of our weaknesses. But He also knows all the answers and has cleared *the Way* to get all of our prayers answered. We need to enter into prayer with a full assurance of faith. We must be completely confident in His desire and ability to answer our prayers.

*Therefore, brethren, having boldness to enter the Holiest by the blood of Jesus, by a new and living way which He consecrated for us, through the veil, that is, His flesh, and having a High Priest over the house of God, let us draw near with a true heart in **full assurance of faith**, having our hearts sprinkled from an evil conscience and our bodies washed with pure water. Let us hold fast the confession of our hope without wavering, for He who promised is faithful* (Hebrews 10:19-23).

The apostle Paul told the people of Athens, as recorded in the book of Acts, that He is not far from each one of us, for in Him we live and move and have our being (see Acts 17:28). We do not need to do anything that requires difficulty. We just must accept who He is and seek Him earnestly. He wants us to find Him (see Heb. 11:6). Jesus will take care of us. He is the Gate through whom we must enter in order to have a successful prayer life. He is going to bless us abundantly as we pray His purpose for our lives. His purpose for us is an abundant life in every area.

I tell you the truth, I am the gate for the sheep. All who came before me were thieves and robbers. But the true sheep did not listen to them. Yes, I am the gate. Those who come in through me will be saved. They will come and go freely and will find good pastures. The thief's purpose is to steal and kill and destroy. My purpose is to give them a rich and satisfying life (John 10:7-10 NLT).

Chapter 3

THE HOLY SPIRIT IS THE COUNSELOR IN PRAYER

Wonderful Counselor

Jesus is called the *Counselor* in Isaiah 9:6, as well as other names such as *Wonderful, Mighty God, Everlasting Father,* and *Prince of Peace.* One of the names of the Holy Spirit is also *Counselor.*

> But the Comforter (**Counselor**, Helper, Intercessor, Advocate, Strengthener, Standby), *the Holy Spirit, Whom the Father will send in My name [in My place, to represent Me and act on My behalf], He will teach you all things. And He will cause you to recall* (will remind you of, bring to your remembrance) *everything I have told you* (John 14:26 AMPC).

So you can see that you have a great deal of help spiritually when we pray. Both Jesus and the Holy Spirit will counsel you. You should have no problem with your prayer life with all this help.

> *The Spirit of God is calling you to a greater encounter with Him.*

Have you ever wondered how wise the Holy Spirit is? He cannot be taught or counseled.

> *Who has directed the Spirit of the Lord, or as His counselor has taught Him? With whom did He take counsel, and who instructed Him, and taught Him in the path of justice? Who taught Him knowledge, and showed Him the way of understanding? Behold, the nations are as a drop in a bucket, and are counted as the small dust on the scales; look, He lifts up the isles as a very little thing* (Isaiah 40:13-15).

We need to remind ourselves continuously that the Holy Spirit is God. When we are ready to yield to Him in prayer, we are going to see things differently than we ever saw them before our encounter with God. We will see things differently when we fully yield to Him. Our eyes of understanding will be opened as we begin to see into the Spirit realm. Some very important events will occur when we decide to enter in with Him.

The Spirit of God is calling you to a greater encounter with Him. He longs to coach you into the activities of Heaven and manifest them on the earth. It is time for you to allow the Holy One to take you into prayer conquests with Him. Together you will mix faith with what the Spirit is saying and begin to speak it out in the physical realm. Your spiritual eyes see the invisible as you begin to pray out the mysteries of God and see your prayers answered. Be filled with power as you confirm God's intention for you with the utterance that comes from God's own heart.

The Holy Spirit is called the "Spirit of Jesus Christ." The Spirit will take what Jesus says and make it known to you. He wants to reveal Jesus and empower us to live and testify of Him. The Holy Spirit will manifest Himself in and through you. He has been sent to counsel you in your daily activities as you live for God's purpose. You have to understand that the Holy Spirit wants to promote Jesus and make "Christ in you" a full reality.

> *For I know that this will turn out for my deliverance through your prayer and the supply of the Spirit of Jesus Christ, according to my earnest expectation and hope that in nothing I shall be ashamed, but with all boldness, as always, so now also Christ will be magnified in my body, whether by life or by death. For to me, to live is Christ, and to die is gain. But if I live on in the flesh, this will mean fruit from my labor; yet what I shall choose I cannot tell* (Philippians 1:19-22).

The Spirit of Christ lives in you. He wants to be magnified and produce fruit through your life on earth. Jesus, through the Holy Spirit, will cause your prayer life to prosper! Remember that you must be willing to yield to the Spirit. Jesus said to pray! "Then He came to the disciples and found them sleeping, and said to Peter, 'What! Could you not watch with Me one hour? Watch and pray, lest you enter into temptation. *The spirit indeed is willing, but the flesh is weak*'" (Matt. 26:40-41). Let us learn from the disciples and stir ourselves up and enter into prayer, and then we will receive answers! The Kingdom is advancing at an incredible rate. With or without you, Jesus is leading His sons and daughters to victory through prayer. Here is what the Spirit is saying to you right now:

If you will choose to step into the Spirit this day, I will lead you into the reality, the purpose I have for you. In My Kingdom, I have plans for you that cannot fail. If you will only yield and pray Heaven's prayers and pray them with Heaven's purpose, all would be well with you as you discover your destiny in Me.

One of the most powerful characteristics of the Holy Spirit is that He is Truth. The Holy Spirit's truth can be translated as the Spirit of reality. Facts can be wrong, but the truth is always reality. This is the Spirit who helps you when you do not know how to pray.

He is the Holy Spirit, who leads into all truth. The world cannot receive him, because it isn't looking for him and doesn't recognize him. But you know him, because he lives with you now and later will be in you. No, I will not abandon you as orphans—I will come to you. Soon the world will no longer see me, but you will see me. Since I live, you also will live (John 14:17-19 NLT).

Also, when He comes, Jesus said that He would speak what He heard the Father say and tell us the future.

All that belongs to the Father is mine; this is why I said, "The Spirit will tell you whatever he receives from me" (John 16:15 NLT).

That is why we must yield to the Holy Spirit when we enter into prayer conquests. He knows the future and will remind us of the truth that Jesus taught us. He is a lawyer who has never lost a case as long as people who were His clients acted completely submissive and yielding to His advice.

But when the Father sends the Advocate as my representative—that is, the Holy Spirit—he will teach you everything

44

and will remind you of everything I have told you (John 14:26 NLT).

The Joy Is Coming

In the book of John, Jesus explained one of the first manifestations of the Spirit of God that people will experience in their prayer life. He explained that the disciples' sorrow was about to be turned to joy that could not be taken away. Jesus told them that they would receive that for which they ask and that they will have abundant joy.

> *So you have sorrow now, but I will see you again; then you will rejoice, and **no one can rob you of that joy**. At that time you won't need to ask me for anything. I tell you the truth, you will ask the Father directly, and he will grant your request because you use my name. You haven't done this before. Ask, using my name, and you will receive, and **you will have abundant joy** (John 16:22-24 NLT).*

Three Other Works of the Spirit

> *But if I go away, I will send Him to you [to be in close fellowship with you]* (John 16:7 AMPC).

In John 16, we read how the Holy Spirit desires to be intimate with us in friendship. He will definitely enhance our prayer life with this type of relationship. However, there are three other things He does that will also affect us. One thing that is influenced is your environment as it *deals with the world*. We are not of this world, but we are in it. We are the salt of the earth, as Jesus says (see Matt. 5:13).

When the Spirit arrives on the scene, He will do three major things that will cause a reaction in the spirit realm and rock the world in which you live. So be prepared for the shift! John 16:8 says that when He arrives:

> *He will convict and convince the world and bring demonstra-tion to it about sin and about righteousness* (uprightness of heart and right standing with God) *and about judg-ment: about **sin**, because they do not believe in Me [trust in, rely on, and adhere to Me]; about **righteousness*** (upright-ness of heart and right standing with God), *because I go to My Father, and you will see Me no longer; about **judg-ment**, because the ruler* (evil genius, prince) *of this world [Satan] is judged and condemned and sentence already is passed upon him* (AMPC).

Chapter 4

SPIRITUAL CONFRONTATION

Sound Doctrine

It is of utmost importance that you understand this next aspect of prayer. Prayer is also an act of confrontation. Sin, righteousness, and judgment are involved in prayer. These three demonstrations of the Spirit of God create a situation of confrontation in prayer. The Holy Spirit does not hold back concerning who He is and what He represents. Do not take it personally if you find yourself on the wrong side of people or circumstances when the Holy Spirit shows up to help you. He has already picked sides, and you must follow Him in regard to sin, righteousness, and judgment. The Kingdom of God is advancing, and confrontation is inevitable. Side with the Holy Spirit and you will find victory in your prayer conquests. God wants to answer your prayers—always. Remember that you must confront the world and the "evil one" with the truth. This is also the work of the Holy Spirit, even if it is seldom mentioned in the Scriptures. Jesus said, "If I cast out demons with the finger of God, surely the kingdom of God has come upon you" (Luke 11:20). It is a sign of the times when we do not hear the full counsel of God from the Word. Paul warned us to be ready for this kind warfare. In the book of 2 Timothy, he told us what to expect:

> *For the time will come when they will not endure sound doctrine, but according to their own desires, because they have itching ears, they will heap up for themselves teachers; and they will turn their ears away from **the truth**, and be turned aside to fables. But you be watchful in all things, **endure afflictions**, do the work of an evangelist, fulfill your ministry* (2 Timothy 4:3-5).

I have to tell everyone concerning prayer that the most blatant, strong, and yet hidden and deceptive form of warfare that the enemy uses against us is what the military calls a *disinformation campaign*. Disinformation is false information deliberately and often covertly spread (for example, by the planting of rumors) in order to influence public opinion or obscure the truth.

> *If you really want to combat evil spirits, then label, pull down, and expose everything they say and do. Then, by binding and driving them out of your midst, you have done successful warfare.*

It is helpful to remember that satan is called the father of lies because he employs lies to try to have victory over us. We wrestle with the lies of the enemy not only in our minds but also in our dealings with the unredeemed. Unfortunately, we also wrestle with the enemy's lies within the church as a whole. It is not a new mode of operation that the enemy is using. He used it on Eve in the Garden of Eden. He deceived Adam with lies also. The enemy lied to Adam and Eve to make them think that God had somehow excluded them from something they needed. He also had them questioning what God really said and meant. Remember that our enemy is a spirit. Paul told the Ephesians:

> Be strong in the Lord and in the power of His might. Put on the whole armor of God, that you may be able to stand against the wiles of the devil. For we do not wrestle against flesh and blood, but against principalities, against powers, against the rulers of the darkness of this age, against **spiritual hosts of wickedness in the heavenly places**. Therefore take up the whole armor of God, that you may be able to withstand in the evil day, and having done all, to stand (Ephesians 6:10-13).

If you really want to combat evil spirits, then label, pull down, and expose everything they say and do. Then, by binding and driving them out of your midst, you have done successful warfare. Then you must educate everyone involved with the truth to bring deliverance so that the enemy cannot come back and rebuild. This is a part of prayer and must be discussed. Paul clearly defines spiritual warfare in the letter to the Corinthians:

> For though we walk in the flesh, we do not war according to the flesh. For the weapons of our warfare are not carnal but mighty in God for pulling down strongholds, casting down arguments and every high thing that exalts itself against the knowledge of God, bringing every thought into captivity to the obedience of Christ, and being ready to punish all disobedience when your obedience is fulfilled (2 Corinthians 10:3-6).

Your Relationship Will Confront Devils

Fellowship

Paul told the Philippians that if they encountered any consolation in Christ or "fellowship of the Spirit" to fulfill his joy by *"being like-minded"* (Phil. 2:1-4). There is a fellowship of the wonderful, majestic Holy Spirit that every believer should seek to encounter. This will enhance your walk with God by developing this aspect of fellowship in your relationship with Him. Consider what influence the Holy Spirit will have on you in your everyday life. More importantly, consider the Holy Spirit's influence on your prayer life. I know that He helps me to pray when I feel that I cannot pray. When I sense that He wants to say something to me, sometimes He is nudging me to say something as well. This gives God permission to act on behalf of others, as well as me, when I speak out. There is a legal side to prayer because we have authority through Jesus Christ. God the Father knows that Jesus has given the keys of the Kingdom to each believer and to the church. This is what happens during *fellowship of the Spirit*:

1. Fellowship of the Spirit allows dialogue, or conversation, to occur.

2. Fellowship of the Spirit reveals the true intent of our hearts.

3. Fellowship of the Spirit gives utterance—a voice—to our desires.

4. Fellowship of the Spirit brings about unity in our mission and purpose.

5. Fellowship of the Spirit executes justice when our agreement is accomplished.

6. Fellowship of the Spirit will result in the commission of angels to accomplish what has been agreed upon on our behalf.

7. Fellowship of the Spirit manifests good fruit in and through us.

8. Fellowship of the Spirit advances the Kingdom of God, which is the King on the earth. Everyone who participates enjoys the spoils and benefits of that fellowship.

Communion

Communion is about the love of God. It brings about intimacy, adoration, and worship. Deep secrets are revealed. You allow yourself to be vulnerable. You gain each other's strengths and absorb any weaknesses so that they are no longer issues. We can define *communion* as intimate fellowship, rapport, or communication. *Communication* is the act or process of using words, sounds, signs, or behaviors to express or exchange information or ideas, thoughts, feelings, etc. to someone else.

Paul talked about the love of God and the communion of the Holy Spirit toward the Corinthians (see 2 Cor. 13:14). We need to have this kind of relationship with the Holy Spirit while we are on the earth. The Spirit will start to communicate with us about our destiny that is already recorded in Heaven. We will start to walk out every intention of God for our lives. We will find ourselves influencing others to do the same. We need to be strong in the Lord and the power of His might (see Eph. 6:10).

Stop Grieving the Holy Spirit

Last, we must not grieve the Holy Spirit by what we do and say in our life. If He is grieved, it is because we strayed from our path of destiny.

If I have grieved the Spirit of God, I have lost the edge to my communion and fellowship with Him. If I sense that the Spirit has pulled back in sorrow, I know that this will hinder my prayer life. Effective prayer that gets results occurs when the Holy Spirit is in agreement with you and you will have confidence and full assurance of faith. The apostle Paul said, "And do not bring sorrow to God's Holy Spirit by the way you live. Remember, he has identified you as his own, guaranteeing that you will be saved on the day of redemption" (Eph. 4:30 NLT).

Some things to remember about the Holy Spirit and Jesus when you pray are:

1. The Spirit alone gives life to your prayers. He is the One who gives eternal life.

2. Human effort accomplishes nothing.

3. The very words that Jesus has spoken and that you repeat in prayer are Spirit and life.

4. Some do not believe Jesus's words, and that can be a hindrance to your prayers (see John 6:63-64).

I remember, just recently, when my relationship with God had caused confrontation in the realm of the Spirit. I was praying in tongues and exercising my authority in the name of Jesus. This activity caused an amazing visitation from an angel. It occurred at the beginning of 2016, right before our spiritual parents, Dr. Jesse and Dr. Cathy Duplantis, ordained my wife and me. The devil was already contesting this ordination, even though we were not aware that it was going to happen yet. I had been praying in the Spirit for close to three days, almost continually, and had not been able to sleep. I felt such a burden to pray in the Spirit. I could not stop even though I tried. Finally, on the third night, I was lying on my bed praying quietly in the Spirit, in order to not disturb my wife, when a very loud gust of wind came from outside my house window. I could hear the trees rustling in the wind as things were blowing around outside the house. I thought, "There must be a storm coming in." Just as that thought passed through my mind, I heard a large tree branch break and fall to the ground. As it crashed, I sat up abruptly to see what was happening out my window.

As I looked out the window, which I could do without getting up from the bed, I was surprised to see that there was no wind at all and that there were no broken branches on the ground in my yard. As I looked in disbelief, I saw that the clouds were parting. The bright moon was shining through, giving light to the yard. There was no visible sign of what I was hearing. That is when I noticed an outline of a person coming toward me between the clouds in the air at a high rate of speed. The clouds were parting, giving way to him as he came and touched down, feet first on the golf course behind my house. Then, he came running toward my house.

He walked right into the house and came up from behind me and picked me up off my feet with my back resting against his chest. As he lifted me higher, I could feel his left cheek and my right cheek touching. He had put his arms through and around me. He was at least eight feet tall and had a massive build. As I was dangling in mid-air, in a bear hug, he breathed in. I could feel his chest expand. He said he had come in answer my prayers. In front of us, since he arrived, demonic forces had become visible. He said, "Where we live, on the other side, this is how we angels deal with demonic forces." I could see, in the spirit, the whole way to the city of New Orleans, which is about 20 miles away. There were three demonic entities that were sent to attack us at our house. I could see that they were already within striking distance of our neighborhood. As he exhaled the breath of God that he had previously inhaled, the demons were sent tumbling backward. They went the entire distance back to New Orleans without even a battle ensuing! He then set me down and turned to fly away.

He was gone as fast as he had come, but the effects of the encounter have not left me. I will always remember that my prayers were heard. I know that I must continually exercise my authority as a believer. Angels will be sent to answer our prayers and assist us in an awesome, supernatural way when we exercise the authority that God has imparted to us.

Chapter 5

THE HOLY SPIRIT: THE BREATH OF HEAVEN

Allowing the Holy Spirit to Move upon You in Prayer

Have you ever imagined what it was like when the "mighty rushing wind" came on the Day of Pentecost? I have, and the same type of great move of God is starting again because Heaven is visiting us in these last days. The Holy Spirit is the Master of the spirit realm. The supernatural is the Holy Spirit's everyday environment. The breath of God and the Holy Spirit are one. Jesus even breathed on His disciples one day and said, "Receive the Holy Spirit."

As we learn about the mighty Holy Spirit, remember that He is to be treated as part of the Godhead. He is part of the Godhead and is expressed through wind, breath, fire, gifts, a dove, a liberator, an attorney, power, and authority—just to name a few. But remember, He is a person and part of the Holy Trinity, and He can be grieved. He is known in the Kingdom for righteousness, peace, and joy. Paul said, "For the kingdom of God is not eating and drinking, but righteousness and peace and joy in the Holy Spirit. For he who serves Christ in these things is acceptable to God and approved by men" (Rom. 14:17-18). When we pray in the Holy Spirit, we are in the Kingdom of God. The one who prays and is accepted by God serves in these three things—righteousness, peace, and joy in the Holy Spirit. When Jesus taught me to pray, He showed me that I would encounter these three attributes, as well as the *resurrection power* that raised Jesus from the dead (see Eph. 2:5).

> *Now is the time to allow Him to pray out*
> *the mysteries of God through you!*

The Spirit Living in You

When I pray under the influence of the Holy Spirit, I can sense the powers of the coming age spoken of in the book of Hebrews (see Heb. 6:5). This working of power has the ability to influence every part of your being. The mighty power will enable you to pray yourself into your answer.

As you yield to the mighty Holy Spirit, He is taking you on to greater heights. These heights are where you can stand within His ability. You are able to see into the future that you could not see before moving into these heights. Your view was obstructed due to your former vantage point. He will unveil your purpose—that purpose which was recorded long ago. Your purpose was written from the Father's heart for you and now is revealed by the Holy Spirit. Yield to the Spirit of the living God and you will pray in a way that moves you into your destiny. Do not delay the entrance into the spirit realm. Pray and yield to that which the Spirit is saying. Now is the time to allow Him to pray out the mysteries of God through you!

The Holy Spirit has the capability of raising people from the dead. He was the One who was involved in that process. Jesus told me when I had my *heavenly visitation* that He had such a relationship with the Father God and the Holy Spirit that He had to trust them when He died and went to hell. For the full account of this story, please see my previous book entitled *Heavenly Visitation*. He said with a broken voice, "I had to trust that the Father would give the command on the third day for the Holy Spirit to raise Me from the dead." The power of the Holy Spirit broke Him out of the hellish prison and brought Him back to life in His earthly body. He is the Resurrection and the Life. The Holy Spirit was the person who enabled Christ to rise to life. So when you pray, you must remember that very same power is available and effectual when we pray fervently (see James 5:16).

We have the life of God in us. He wants to pray through us. He will quicken us. "The Spirit of God, who raised Jesus from the dead, lives in you. And just as God raised Christ Jesus from the dead, he will give life to your mortal bodies by this same Spirit living within you" (Rom. 8:11 NLT). It is time for the Holy Spirit to get our bodies energized with the life of God. Let faith rise up in our heart and tell our soul to trust in God.

> *Why are you cast down, O my soul? And why are you disquieted within me? Hope in God, for I shall yet praise Him for the help of His countenance* (Psalm 42:5).

Being Filled with the Spirit

It is very important to be filled with the Spirit of God. Let Him continually flow as rivers of living water out of you as you begin to pray in the Spirit (see John 7:38).

Therefore do not be unwise, but understand what the will of the Lord is. And do not be drunk with wine, in which is dissipation; but be filled with the Spirit, speaking to one another in Psalm and hymns and spiritual songs, singing and making melody in your heart to the Lord, giving thanks always for all things to God the Father in the name of our Lord Jesus Christ, submitting to one another in the fear of God (Ephesians 5:17-21).

Six characteristics of someone living a Spirit-filled life are:

1. They understand what the Lord's will for their life is.

2. They are not drunk with wine, but are filled with the Spirit.

3- They speak to one another in psalms, hymns, and spiritual songs.

4. They sing and make melody in their heart to the Lord.

5. They give thanks to their Father God.

6. They submit to one another in the fear of God.

The apostle Paul was filled with the Holy Spirit. It was a separate occasion from his salvation experience (see Acts 9:3-9). He met the Lord Christ on horseback on his way to persecute more Christians. He later had another, second experience with the Holy Spirit.

And Ananias went his way and entered the house; and laying his hands on him he said, "Brother Saul, the Lord Jesus, who appeared to you on the road as you came, has sent me that you may receive your sight and **be filled with the Holy Spirit**" (Acts 9:17).

From that point on, Paul spoke in tongues. He was always bold because he was filled with the Holy Spirit. He told the Corinthians, "I thank God that I speak in tongues more than any of you" (1 Cor. 14:18 NLT). Speaking in tongues is something that Jesus has told me is *the single most important activity in which a Christian can participate.* (Please see the full account on this subject in my book *Heavenly Visitation.*)

I remember an important concept that the Lord revealed to me several years ago. We were assisting a pastor friend who was starting a church in our city. During our weekly prayer meeting, the Spirit of God showed me what was possible if I yielded to Him during prayer.

The prayer time was held at our house regularly. On this particular occasion, practically the whole congregation showed up to pray. We were scattered throughout the living room, dining room, and kitchen. I was going from room to room, which was my custom at times, in order to encourage people to pray with greater focus and intensity.

As we were praying, I suddenly felt the breath of Heaven come over me. I immediately felt an unction inside to pray more forcefully. I continued to go around to each individual and pray in my heavenly language referred by the apostle Paul as "speaking in tongues." However, without warning, as I would pass certain individuals my prayer language in tongues would switch to English. I would give them instruction with a fluent boldness that could only come from Heaven itself. It went on that way until most of the attendees had received a word from the Spirit. What was amazing was that in between transitioning from one individual to the next, I would revert back to praying in tongues until I came upon the next individual. I had no idea what I was doing at the time.

Toward the end of the prayer meeting, I found myself in the kitchen, standing there, wrapped in the glory of God. The house and its occupants disappeared without a trace as I was caught up in a vision. I could not see anything except the glory brightly shining around me. That glory appeared as if it were piles of diamonds reflecting a bright light source. I heard the Lord say, "In My presence, there are no shadows." I looked down, and I could not see the floor of my house. There were no shadows, no matter at what angle I looked. He told me that there are no questions, just answers, when you stand with Him.

I then came back to my house. The prayer meeting was closing. As everyone was visiting, one by one people were coming up to me and telling me what happened to them during the time of prayer. I was shocked! They told me how I was going around, praying in tongues and switching to English. What I did not know was that when I spoke in English, I was giving them the answer to the prayer that they were uttering to God. I could not hear their prayers, but God did, and He was answering them by the Spirit through me!

> *Remember that the breath of Heaven helps you pray. Your answer is already on the way as your prayer leaves your lips!*

Chapter 6

Walking in Him and Your Effectiveness in Prayer

The Three Parts of Man

One important aspect of our makeup, as God has created us, is the three parts of our person. We have a permanent existence because of our origin as an eternal living spiritual being; that is our spirit, which originated in the heart of God. We also possess a soul, which includes our mind, our will, and our emotions. Lastly, we possess a body, which is our "earth suit."

> *May your whole spirit, soul, and body be preserved blameless* (1 Thessalonians 5:23).

The apostle Paul revealed the three parts of man to us in his writings to believers in the New Testament. He mentioned *spirit, soul, and body* to the Thessalonians. In addition to the Corinthians, he explained in great detail about the differences between all three.

*All things are lawful for me, but all things are not helpful. All things are lawful for me, but I will not be brought under the power of any. Foods for the stomach and the stomach for foods, but God will destroy both it and them. Now the body is not for sexual immorality but for the Lord, and the Lord for the body. And God both raised up the Lord and will also raise us up by His power. Do you not know that your bodies are members of Christ? Shall I then take the members of Christ and make them members of a harlot? Certainly not! Or do you not know that he who is joined to a harlot is one body with her? For "the two," He says, "shall become one flesh." But he who is joined to the Lord is one spirit with Him. Flee sexual immorality. Every sin that a man does is outside the body, but he who commits sexual immorality sins against his own body. Or do you not know that your body is the temple of the Holy Spirit who is in you, whom you have from God, and **you are not your own**? For you were bought at a price; therefore glorify God in your **body** and in your **spirit**, which are God's* (1 Corinthians 6:12-20).

The spirit of man is the first important aspect we must consider when discussing walking in the Spirit. We must first realize that the Holy Spirit must have a way of becoming one with man spiritually. The fact that we can walk in the spirit is proof that man actually is a spiritual being who is eternal as well as flesh and blood.

Origin of Man

God is eternal because He did not come from the physical realm but the original realm—the realm of the Spirit. There has never been time, as we know it, in the realm of the Spirit. In Heaven, there is no aging as there is on earth. As an eternal Spirit, God said, "Let Us make man in Our image, after Our likeness.... So God created man in His own image; in the image of God He created him" (Gen. 1:26-27).

So man is made in the image of God. We are to worship Him in spirit and in truth because He is a Spirit and we are a spirit (see John 4:24). Man was created in His likeness so man is also a spirit as well. God gave man a soul, and he lives in a body (see 1 Thess. 5:23). The spirit of man will separate from the body and be with Christ when we leave this earth realm to be with Him in Heaven, if we are born again.

> *For I am in a strait betwixt two, having a desire to depart, and to be with Christ; which is far better: nevertheless to abide in the flesh is more needful for you* (Philippians 1:23-24 KJV).

> *But though our outward man perish, yet the inward man is renewed day by day* (2 Corinthians 4:16 KJV).

> *The fact that we can walk in the spirit is proof that man actually is a spiritual being who is eternal as well as flesh and blood.*

The Born-Again Spirit of Man

Jesus said to Nicodemus, "Except a man be born again, he cannot see the kingdom of God" (John 3:3 KJV). Jesus was talking about spiritual birth, not physical birth. Nicodemus reacted as most people do. "How can a man be born when he is old? Can he enter a second time into his mother's womb and be born?" (John 3:4). This is the thought process of many. Their initial reaction is toward the natural, not toward the spiritual. Jesus differentiated between the physical and the spiritual when He said, *"That which is born of the flesh is flesh, and that which is born of the Spirit is spirit"* (John 3:6).

The apostle Peter wrote that your spirit is the "hidden man of the heart," which is not corruptible but of a meek and quiet spirit. "But let it be the hidden man of the heart, in that which is not corruptible, even the ornament of a meek and quiet spirit, which is in the sight of God of great price" (1 Peter 3:4 KJV). The born-again spirit of man is so restored to the image of God that if we will seek to be of a meek and quiet spirit, we will not experience corruption. The hidden man of the heart is in communication with God. We who are led by the Spirit of God are not led with our heads or our feelings. In the same way, our bodies do not lead those of us who are led by the Spirit. It is only through our spirit, when we are a new creature in Christ, that the Spirit of God can lead us.

Led by the Spirit of God

Many people are led by their own desires and do not even know it because they are dominated by the flesh. This kind of life becomes selfish and works against the desires of the Spirit. It hurts the Kingdom because other people are affected as well. The Spirit of God can be grieved, and this grieving will cause Him to pull back. As believers, we should desire what the Spirit wants and yield to Him. "For as many as are led by the Spirit of God, these are the sons of God" (Rom. 8:14).

Children of God

The Spirit of God has announced that we are children of God. It is through our spirit, the spirit within us, that the Holy Spirit communicates to us. "The Spirit Himself bears witness with our spirit that we are children of God" (Rom. 8:16). Your see, the Holy Spirit of God is speaking from His Spirit to our spirit. As children of our Father God, we receive every provision from the spiritual realm. These things then manifest into this earthly realm by the reality that comes from this manifestation in our spirits. "Now faith is the substance of things hoped for, the evidence of things not seen" (Heb. 11:1). The Spirit of God knows no defeat. He knows not how to doubt. It is foreign to Him. It is not in the communication of heaven. Paul said:

> When I was a child, I spoke as a child, I understood as a child, I thought as a child; but when I became a man, I put away childish things. For now we see in a mirror, dimly, but then face to face. Now I know in part, but then I shall know just as I also am known (1 Corinthians 13:11-12).

So now, the only way we can see and hear is by the spirit realm; we see and hear spirit to Spirit. When we lose this flesh and blood body and our fleshly mind, which is our carnal understanding, we will be able to see and hear clearly without any hindrance.

The Candle of the Lord

David's son Solomon, in all his wisdom, concluded that the heart of man or his spirit is lit up like a candle or a light bulb. "The spirit of man is the candle of the Lord, searching all the inward parts of the belly" (Prov. 20:27 KJV). This is a good verse to talk about when gaining understanding about how the human spirit works with the Holy Spirit. The spirit of man is like a light that illuminates all the inward parts. We only have to yield to the Holy Spirit as He illuminates our inward parts. This light will illuminate our path and allow us to see clearly each step to take in the Lord's perfect will. When the Lord would light David's candle, referring to his spirit, in the Old Testament, David was able to see and the darkness was dispelled. David said, "For thou wilt light my candle: the Lord my God will enlighten my darkness" (Ps. 18:28 KJV). So you can see that the human spirit has the ability to encounter the Holy Spirit so powerfully that it creates light from Heaven in your heart. That light allows us to have a wonderful, intimate communication from Heaven. The apostle John says that when we walk in the light, the result is fellowship with Him.

> But if we walk in the light as He is in the light, we have fellowship with one another, and the blood of Jesus Christ His Son cleanses us from all sin (1 John 1:7).

Spirit Consciousness

John 4:24 says, "God is Spirit, and those who worship Him must worship in Spirit and truth." If our God is Spirit, then we must contact Him with our spirit. This means that our spirit has the ability to communicate with God's Spirit. We change our way of thinking in order to understand that God communicates with us.

> But as it is written: "Eye has not seen, nor ear heard, nor have entered into the heart of man the things which God has prepared for those who love Him." But God has revealed them to us through His Spirit. For the Spirit searches all things, yes, the deep things of God. For what man knows the things of a man except the spirit of the man which is in him? Even so no one knows the things of God except the Spirit of God. Now we have received, not the spirit of the world, but the Spirit who is from God, that we might know the things that have been freely given to us by God. These things we also speak, not in words which man's wisdom teaches but which the Holy Spirit teaches, comparing spiritual things with spiritual. But the natural man does not receive the things

of the Spirit of God, for they are foolishness to him; nor can he know them, because they are spiritually discerned. But he who is spiritual judges all things, yet he himself is rightly judged by no one. For "who has known the mind of the Lord that he may instruct Him?" But we have the mind of Christ (1 Corinthians 2:9-16).

This is a profound passage of Scripture that we can meditate upon for a long time and probably still not get everything out of it that the Holy Spirit intended. Here we must understand that God is giving us secrets about many things. In order to pray effectively, we must team up with the One who has been sent to help us pray. If someone was sent to help you in an area and that person was an expert in his or her field, you would submit to their counsel and abilities. You would allow your task to begin and to end with their oversight. So let us see what the truth is about our situation concerning where we stand now and where the Spirit of Counsel wants to take us.

> *On our own, we do not know what God has prepared for us who love Him! How can we pray without Him?*

First Paul, by the Holy Spirit, lets us know our condition and what we lack without the Counselor. According to Scripture, here is our condition:

Our Condition

1. Your eyes have not seen.

We need to realize that in our condition, and without the Holy Spirit's help, our eyes may have the ability to see, but we are not able to *discern* the spiritual realities before us. It is apparent when our eyes become spiritually opened—we will be able to see spiritual realities more clearly.

2. Your ears have not heard.

We need our spiritual ears open as well. Our spiritual ears need to be able to pick up the voice of Heaven and discern what is being said to those who have *ears that hear.*

3. Your mind has not imagined.

God gave us the ability to imagine. Our mind can make an image of anything it wants. We have the ability to do what we imagined. At the time of the Tower of Babel, the Trinity decided to come down to see the city and the tower the Babylonians had built.

> And the Lord said, Behold, the **people is one**, and they have all one language; and this they begin to do: and now **nothing will be restrained** from them, which they have **imagined** to do. Go to, let us go down, and there confound their language, that they may not understand one another's speech (Genesis 11:6-7 KJV).

But the apostle Paul tells us that our mind has not even imagined what God has for us. We need the Spirit to help us.

4. It has not entered into your heart.

The heart is the deepest part of you, where your passion is found. You cannot even experience the truth in the deepest inner part of you, which is your spirit, until the Spirit of God delivers it to you. Then, and only then, can you truly see what God has planned for you. When the spiritual reality finally enters through the gates of your heart, you will be flooded with understanding.

Thank God Paul does not stop there. The apostle tells us that *through the Spirit of God* we can receive revelation of what *He has for us.*

Knowing what God has for us is the knowledge of His will for our life. I do not know about you, but I perceive that it is invaluable to know what plans God has for me.

I recall a time when I wanted to discern God's will and could not get clarity. It concerned some leadership training that I was asked to attend for my church. It would require me to miss work. That meant the time for training would cost me a whole week's wages because it involved a long weekend. My job required me to travel and I worked on an airplane for three days at a time, so I would have to lose the whole three-day trip. I remember entering an elevator at the hotel in Pittsburgh, Pennsylvania and asking the Lord again what I should do. I had asked the Lord for the answer to this same question several weeks prior with no answer. This time, I stated my case and felt that I should at least have the conference paid by the church because I was losing a week's wages to attend the required training. I received no answer to my prayer, so I continued to my room and flew out the next day to complete my work week at the airline.

The next week I was in the very same hotel. As I stepped into the elevator, I realized that God had not yet answered. So I stated my case again, including the fact that He should compensate me for the cost of the conference, which was a little over a hundred dollars. As I got off the elevator, I still did not hear Him say anything. I got my key out, placed it in the door, and entered my room for the night. Immediately, I heard what was apparently the audible voice of God. He told me to get on my knees immediately. I thought I was in trouble, so I started to repent. *I am sorry for complaining, Lord,* I said. In an audible voice, He said, "Look under your bed." There, under my bed, was a one hundred dollar bill. There was a great deal of garbage under there also. The hundred dollar bill was very old. But I began to thank God for it and asked Him if I should change it into twenties because it looked so old and did not seem authentic to me. He told me it was real, and I put in my pocket.

The next morning as I was boarding my flight, a gentleman who was carrying a firearm with the proper paperwork checked in with me. This was the proper procedure for all armed individuals on an aircraft. He was with the Department of the Treasury counterfeit division. I saw that the Lord was providing me with the confirmation I needed concerning my one hundred dollar bill, so I pulled the bill out of my pocket and showed it to him. He said that it was old, but it was authentic. God had answered my prayer and the gentleman went and sat down in his seat. God had confirmed to me His will. He provided the needed money and a confirmation of the authenticity of the one hundred dollar bill. I use this story as an example of the fact that God does answer our prayers and that we also must be specific with Him. The Holy Spirit will give us revelation on how to pray.

> *God's revelation through His Holy Spirit helps you pray effectively.*

Whenever I pray, I ask the Holy Spirit to make known God's will and His intention for me through His written Word. Next, I ask that the revelation of God's Word would flow through my spirit and out of my mouth by the Holy Spirit. Finally, when I start to utter words from my lips of what God is saying by His Word and by the Spirit, they flow together in a stream of power. When I make my requests known to God, the peace of God guards my heart because my words match Heaven (see Phil. 4:6-7). I see all of Heaven implement His plan for my life!

Chapter 7

WHAT THE HOLY SPIRIT WANTS YOU TO KNOW

One of the most profound things about my experiences with Jesus, especially during my 1992 visitation when I passed on the operating table, was the many things that I learned with Him that I did not previously understand. I thought that I had knowledge of the Bible and spiritual realities, but I soon found out that I was lacking in some areas. The following passage of Scripture has become my template or road map, if you will, for what I believe the Spirit of God wants everyone to know and fully understand. Please trust me on this—there is so much that we think we understand about the Holy Spirit and spiritual things. After spending time with Jesus and the Holy Spirit, I was sent back with an understanding of the heavenly realms that I did not previous know. In some cases, I was shown things that I knew but I did not want to accept as true. It was sobering to learn that we are absolutely desperate without the help of the Holy Spirit. If we are to learn how to live in two worlds and get our prayers answered, we are going to have to learn the things that the Spirit wants us to know. Here is what I live by. When I was sent back from the dead, I knew that the whole second chapter of 1 Corinthians was to be my template for visitation and prayer. I have included a portion of it here.

> *"No eye has seen, no ear has heard, and no mind has imagined what God has prepared for those who love him." But it was to us that God revealed these things by his Spirit. For his Spirit searches out everything and shows us God's deep secrets. No one can know a person's thoughts except that person's own spirit, and no one can know God's thoughts except God's own Spirit. And we have received God's Spirit (not the world's spirit), so we can know the wonderful things God has freely given us. When we tell you these things, we do not use words that come from human wisdom. Instead, we speak words given to us by the Spirit, using the Spirit's words to explain spiritual truths. But people who aren't spiritual can't receive these truths from God's Spirit. It all sounds foolish to them and they can't understand it, for only those who are spiritual can understand what the Spirit means. Those who are spiritual can evaluate all things, but they themselves cannot be evaluated by others. For, "Who can know the Lord's thoughts? Who knows enough to teach him?" But we understand these things, for we have the mind of Christ (1 Corinthians 2:9-16 NLT).*

1. The Spirit searches all things.

The Holy One has all knowledge and wisdom available to Him. He will access the treasuries and share it with you.

2. *The Spirit searches the deep things of God.*

There are things that you do not know. What is even more profound is the fact that there are things that are yours but you do not even know to ask for them. He will tell you about them and give you faith to ask and receive.

3. *The spirit of the man, which is inside, knows the things about that man.*

Your spirit is the "real you" and knows everything about you. This is the spiritual part of you that lives forever.

4. *No one knows the things of God except the Spirit of God.*

The Holy Spirit is the One from whom you want counsel. He understands the things of God and will make them available to you.

5. *We have not received the spirit of the world.*

The "spirit of the world" is the spirit of the anti-Christ. The "god of this world" is satan. We have not received this wrong, fearful, evil spirit of the world. Jesus said, "If you then, being evil, know how to give good gifts to your children, how much more will your heavenly Father give the Holy Spirit to those who ask Him!" (Luke 11:13).

6. *We have received the Spirit who is from God.*

The Holy Spirit was given in fulfillment of what Jesus, the prophet Joel, and John the Baptist spoke. The apostle Paul told Timothy, "For God has not given us a spirit of fear, but of power and of love and of a sound mind" (2 Tim. 1:7).

7. *We know, by the Spirit, the things that have been freely given to us by God.*

The Spirit of God gives us revelation and empowers us to be witnesses of Him. The apostle Paul told the Corinthian church, "My speech and my preaching were not with persuasive words of human wisdom, *but in demonstration of the Spirit and of power,* that your faith should not be in the wisdom of men but in the power of God" (1 Cor. 2:4-5).

What the Holy Spirit Wants to Teach You

1. *It is not in words that man's wisdom teaches.*

Most of the time, man's wisdom is just from observance and not from the place of the *absolute.* In Heaven, the wisdom is always absolute. Wisdom lives there, alongside absolute truth. The Book of Proverbs explains that wisdom is a person. We need God's wisdom that came down from Heaven—Jesus Christ.

2. *It is words that the Holy Spirit teaches.*

The words that the Holy Spirit teaches are from the Father. He does not speak on His own accord but clearly speaks what the Father tells Him to speak (see John 16:12-15). The Holy One desires to coach you into the supernatural world. The Holy Spirit knows that the supernatural is the natural of Heaven. I know He will lead you step by step into the reality, the truth of His world. Jesus said, *"It is the Spirit who gives life;* the flesh profits nothing. *The words that I speak to you are spirit, and they are life.* But there are some of you who do not believe" (John 6:63-64).

3. *Words comparing spiritual things with spiritual.*

We join together Spirit-revealed truths with Spirit-revealed words (see 1 Cor. 2:13). It's hard to explain something that you know as familiar but that is not familiar to those receiving your message. Your words have to be revelatory for people to grasp the truths. That is why the Spirit of God communicates with your spirit. It is transferred spiritually. Your inner man receives the enlightenment. The mind may not comprehend these spiritual revelations, but your heart rejoices. Eventually, the understanding becomes mentally comprehensible as you continually renew it by the written Word of God!

4. *The natural man does not receive the things of the Spirit of God.*

Most people do not understand the "born-again" experience. When you are born again, you are a brand new creation and your natural self has been made into a very spiritually active species. You cannot accept anything from another realm if you are not enabled to receive the spiritual broadcast from Heaven. You are able to be a good receiver when you are transformed. The signal and its message are placed into your spirit. But if you are spiritually dead because you are in your "natural man" condition, even though the signals from Heaven are broadcast they are not received because you need that new equipment inside of you (see 1 Cor. 2:14).

5. *The words of the Spirit are foolishness to the natural man; he cannot know them because they are spiritually discerned.*

The world and the natural man are not going to participate in the supernatural realm. The Spirit invites you into His realm on His terms. You must be born again and filled with the Holy Spirit to encounter God in His realm.

6. *The man who is spiritual judges all things.*

The spiritual man is discerning and can clearly see to separate between the true and the false. This is because he yields to the Spirit of truth and holiness. He can rightly divide with the sword of the Spirit, the Word of God (see Heb. 4:12).

7. *No one rightly judges the spiritual man.*

A spiritual man makes judgments about all things by the Spirit.

> *But the **spiritual man tries all things** [he examines, **investigates, inquires into, questions, and discerns all things**], yet is himself to be put on trial and judged by no one [he can read the meaning of everything, but no one can properly discern or appraise or get an insight into him]* (1 Corinthians 2:15 AMPC).

You cannot figure out a spiritual person with your carnal mind. Furthermore, an unregenerate person in the world cannot comprehend or see into a spiritual person or relate to his or her world.

8. No one has known the mind of the Lord that he may instruct Him.

The Lord does not need our instruction. We do not know His mind unless He lets us know it! The prophet Isaiah asks:

> *Who has directed the Spirit of the Lord, or as His counselor has taught Him? With whom did He take counsel, that instruction might be given Him? Who taught Him the path of justice and taught Him knowledge and showed Him the way of understanding?* (Isaiah 40:13-14 AMPC)

9. We have the mind of Christ because of the revelation of the Spirit.

It is really good news to know that the Holy Spirit can clearly give us the mind of Jesus. We have revelation and enjoy the walk in the Spirit as we live and experience visitation in prayer.

I am so overcome by the goodness of our God. When I was with Jesus on several occasions, He allowed me to know His heart about certain areas. One of those areas was in the area of God's will. He showed me some things that will help you immensely.

I was taken to a place where I saw the same scenario as the setting of the Bible story of the man at the pool of Bethesda. However, I saw a person in a wheelchair instead. The Lord explained to me that the man at the pool of Bethesda did not know the One with whom he was speaking. He was just telling Jesus his story and wanting someone to put him in the pool when an angel randomly and miraculously stirred the water from time to time. Jesus explained to me that this man did not discern his day of visitation at first. Jesus showed me how people ask for things according to their own knowledge or lack of knowledge, in some cases, of the will of God for their lives. Jesus said that people's failure to understand His will for their lives often limits Him on how He can deal with a person's prayer request. This is because faith is required from all of us as believers. We cannot please God without faith (see Heb. 11:6).

So Jesus explained that if a person were happy with their situation—in this case, confined to a wheelchair—then He would do nothing about it. This shocked me. However, I do know that we receive from God by faith. Jesus then told me even deeper truths that changed my life forever. Jesus said, "Even if they would just want Me to be a friend to them who could visit with them or do some sort of activity with them, I would do that. This is even though I was willing to heal them the whole time. You see, I am limited by their lack of revelation of who I AM." Jesus went on to say, "If they asked Me to get them a meal, I would go and get them whatever they wanted. If they asked Me to push them around in the park, I would do it. I would be whatever they asked of Me according to their faith and knowledge of My will."

This humbled me because many of us are in this situation. We need to discern the will of God in the Word of God by the revelation of the Holy Spirit. He told me that the whole time He was with the man at the pool, He was willing to heal him. How many of us remain in our situation because we do not ask according to the revealed will of God that is found in His Word? Jesus told me that He did not go around making people sick. This was not the Father's revealed will. Instead, God's will was stated in the Book of Acts when Peter said, "How God anointed Jesus of Nazareth with the Holy Spirit and with power, *who went about doing good and healing all who were oppressed by the devil,* for God was with Him" (Acts 10:38). Not only was it revealed that God desires to heal, but Peter also told us who was really behind the sickness—the devil!

Chapter 8

KEEPING IN STEP WITH HIM

There are some very important things that I have to discuss concerning the walk in the supernatural. This will help you with your prayer life immensely. When I was on the other side of the veil with Jesus, He taught me many things that I know I am destined to teach you. Some of these things may be too hard to accept now, but please be prayerful about the subjects anyway.

The intensity of the environment of the heavenly realm is so holy, righteous, and full of the fear of the Lord that most of us would have to start repenting if we encountered it in its fullness. We are so compromised because of the spirit of this world. We have no idea how much influence the forces of evil have on us at times. If we do not consciously seek God with all our heart, with the fear of the Lord present, we are going to be influenced by that spirit whether we want to be influenced or not. I am very touched by what Jesus showed me while I was with Him. I am not always able to talk about some things that I have been taught concerning certain subjects. Between the activities of evil spirits and the weakness of our flesh, the Holy Spirit often gets second or even third place in our lives. In this chapter, I will defend the Holy Spirit. You see, once I died I was left with only Him upon whom to depend. He is all I have. If He is grieved, then I am grieved as well. If He is pleased, then I am pleased. He has become my environment, my source of life. His way of life can cause conflict with your walk down here on the earth.

When we begin to discuss the subject of walking in the Spirit, everyone seems to have his or her own good ideas about what walking in the Spirit really means. I usually have remained silent because, for most people, the cost would be too high if they knew what walking in the Spirit would really mean. Most people believe that Jesus paid the price for them and they don't have to sacrifice anything. I find this very offensive to the Holy Spirit because He knows that simply is not true. If you want to know the Holy Spirit as a person and experience all that the Trinity has written about you, including having all your prayers answered, then you will have to carry your own cross. You will suffer for Him. Yes, Jesus carried the cross and died for you. But He still has told us that we will have to pick up our own cross and follow Him as well. Jesus still believes what He said many years ago and backs it up to this very day. I have been changed to my very core each time I have met with Him.

Jesus wants us to know that it will cost us everything to follow Him. But remember, we will also inherit everything He has in the process as well. This is what Jesus's personality is like when you meet Him as I did. The apostle Mark wrote:

> When He had called the people to Himself, with His disciples also, He said to them, "Whoever desires to come after Me, let him deny himself, and take up his cross, and follow Me. For whoever desires to save his life will lose it,

but whoever loses his life for My sake and the gospel's will save it. For what will it profit a man if he gains the whole world, and loses his own soul? Or what will a man give in exchange for his soul? For whoever is ashamed of Me and My words in this adulterous and sinful generation, of him the Son of Man also will be ashamed when He comes in the glory of His Father with the holy angels" (Mark 8:34-38).

You see, once I died I was left with only Him upon whom to depend. He is all I have. If He is grieved, then I am grieved as well. If He is pleased, then I am pleased. He has become my environment, my source of life. His way of life can cause conflict with your walk down here on the earth.

You see, your experience with the supernatural power of the resurrection has to first have an experience with dying to the flesh and its desires. The flesh can be motivated by evil spirits if it is not crucified. I know we do not hear a lot about this anymore. I want to encounter the supernatural and walk with Him. This is what it takes, and it has to be taught. I know many of you are making the necessary adjustments. This is how you walk with God. Listen to what the apostle Paul says:

I say then: Walk in the Spirit, and you shall not fulfill the lust of the flesh. For the flesh lusts against the Spirit, and the Spirit against the flesh; and these are contrary to one another, so that you do not do the things that you wish. But if you are led by the Spirit, you are not under the law. Now the works of the flesh are evident, which are: adultery, fornication, uncleanness, lewdness, idolatry, sorcery, hatred, contentions, jealousies, outbursts of wrath, selfish ambitions, dissensions, heresies, envy, murders, drunkenness, revelries, and the like; of which I tell you beforehand, just as I also told you in time past, that those who practice such things will not inherit the kingdom of God. But the fruit of the Spirit is love, joy, peace, longsuffering, kindness, goodness, faithfulness, gentleness, self-control. Against such there is no law. And those who are Christ's have crucified the flesh with its passions and desires. If we live in the Spirit, let us also walk in the Spirit. Let us not become conceited, provoking one another, envying one another (Galatians 5:16-26).

The Holy Spirit Wants to Have All of You

1. *Walk in the Spirit, and you will not fulfill the lust of the flesh.*

When we surrender our own will to the Lord and walk humbly with the Holy Spirit, we are opposing the flesh automatically. The Spirit will forbid the flesh to have control if we just continue to submit to His voice and His Word as He reveals them to us. His power will overshadow us as well as spring up within us with resurrection power.

2. *The flesh lusts against the Spirit and the Spirit against the flesh.*

Whatever the agenda, the flesh and the Spirit are against each other. As Christians, it is easy to see the right choice is to follow the Spirit. The Spirit is clearly fighting against the flesh.

3. *The flesh and the Spirit are contrary to one another.*

Always remember that the Spirit always despises the flesh and will never agree until the flesh submits to the Spirit. This requires focus and discipline. The Holy Spirit will teach us the focus and discipline that we need to submit to the Spirit.

4. **When you walk in the Spirit, you do the things that the Spirit desires, which are your heart's desires, but your flesh may not agree with it.**

The desires of your heart will only be given to you as a yielded, born-again believer. If you allow yourself to do so, the flesh will control you. Then you will do things that are contrary to your heart and to the Holy Spirit. However, we will see our prayers answered as we walk in step with the Holy One.

5. **When the Spirit leads you, you are not under the law. You do the will of the Spirit without the law being present.**

The fulfillment of the law is walking in love. Jesus explained to us that we fulfill the law by love. The Spirit of God will always lead you this way and you will do what is right as though the law was present.

I can recall a visitation of Jesus that occurred in 2016. Because of this visitation, it is forever settled concerning His love for me. He is so watchful over me and full of joy when I stay in step with Him by the Holy Spirit. At the beginning of 2016, the Lord asked me to make several decisions that were very hard at the time, but I am now glad that I made those decisions. I know that the Lord wants to protect me, but sometimes you do not see what He does. You have to trust that He knows what is good for you and what is not. Whenever you hear from the Lord, do what He says and you will be promoted. I had to walk to my destiny by faith. This included leaving behind many things I was familiar with. I really was being warned to sever ties with what was old and go into my new destiny. My wife and I continually prayed and fasted until God moved on our behalf. When we heard from God, we did not hesitate to let go of what we could not change. We learned the price that it costs to follow the Lord during this time.

One night, I fell asleep on my side. During the night, I woke up to my name being called. At first it sounded like the Holy Spirit, who was persistently calling my name in order to wake me up. As I opened my eyes, I could see that it was Jesus kneeling by my bed. His face was so close that I had a hard time focusing on Him. He was calling "Kevin!" over and over to get my attention and then passionately and persistently repeating a statement to me. He kept saying to me, "You have to stay in there with Me a little longer. I know it is very difficult right now. Do you understand? A little longer, just stay in there with Me. Do you understand?"

I told Him that I understood. I said, "I understand You because You are eight inches from my face. I hear You." I could see His hairline and all His facial features. That is how close He was to me.

That is when He told me this life-changing statement. "Stay as close and in step with Me as you can. Stay so close that you always have contact with Me shoulder to shoulder. It is going to get easier for you. It is going to break wide open for you very shortly."

I agreed with Him, and He told me some things that would happen as a sign to me. Then He got off His knees and stood upright and walked away. Within two months, things in my life broke open for me, just as Jesus had spoken. I now look at what I had to leave behind as nothing in order to obtain Him. The key to this experience is that He wants us to stay close and walk closely with Him. He is so awesome to behold. I really did not lose anything, but I gained immensely because of my obedience.

Chapter 9

ENEMIES OF THE WALK IN THE SPIRIT

Those who practice such things will not inherit the kingdom of God [let alone get their prayers answered].
—GALATIANS 5:22

Enemies of the Walk in the Spirit

One of the reasons that I did not want to come back from the dead was what I saw on the other side with Jesus. All the evil spirits that were on the earth appalled me. They were assigned to keep human beings in bondage. If the evil spirits succeeded, their victims would either never find out what God had for them, or if they did find out they would be kept in such bondage that they would never break free enough to gain momentum spiritually in order to succeed in God's plan for their life.

I must warn you of what I saw so that you will be set free to serve God with freedom.

I saw that people were encountering all kinds of temptations and hardship that were instigated and carried out by these partly human, partly creature-looking beings. They had no care for their victims and were only interested in destroying the human race. The bad thing about this was that the victims, whether Christian or not, did not know the extent of these evil spirits' involvement.

It seemed to me that Christians' discernment had been dulled to the point where they thought that all the truth in the Bible concerning our enemy is just a fantasy, even though many people would admit that it exists if asked. I realized that most of what people thought and felt was not coming from the Word but from these evil spirits. The sad thing was that they were being influenced to become the very thing that they were not. Getting people to yield to the flesh was the goal of these evil spirits. They were working to get people to act on the impulses of the flesh and speak the lies about themselves and others. The Holy Spirit and the angels were ready to act and push back this darkness, but people had not learned to deny the flesh. Because of pride, they remained in this bondage and never reached their full potential as a believer.

Most unbelievers had absolutely no resistance to the evil spirits or to their flesh that was energized by these rebellious ones. Christians who did not follow the teachings of Jesus were not able to overcome them. They did not discern what had been done for them by God, nor did they discern their own responsibility to submit to God and resist the devil (see James 4:7). Whenever you do not act out in the flesh or speak out through your mouth, because you resisted the evil spirits, is registered as a loss to evil spirits. Paul taught about the works of the flesh and their consequences. These works are your enemies and need to never be made manifest in your life. You can win against these evil spirits by choosing to walk in the Spirit and by taking authority as a believer.

The Evident Works of the Flesh

Here is how Noah Webster defined the terms Paul used to describe the works of the flesh. (These definitions are from the 1828 edition of *Webster's Dictionary*, which is in the public domain.)

1. **Adultery**: "Violation of the marriage bed; a crime, or a civil injury, which introduces, or may introduce, into a family, a spurious offspring."

2. **Fornication**: "The lewdness of unmarried persons, male or female; also, the criminal conversation of a married man with an unmarried woman."

3. **Uncleanness**: "Foulness; dirtiness; filthiness. Be not troublesome to thyself or to others by uncleanness. Want of ritual or ceremonial purity; moral impurity; defilement by sin; sinfulness."

4. **Lewdness**: "The unlawful indulgence of lust; fornication, or adultery. In Scripture, it generally denotes idolatry. Licentiousness; shamelessness."

5. **Idolatry**: "The worship of idols, images, or anything made by hands, or which is not God. Idolatry is of two kinds; the worship of images, statues, pictures, etc. made by hands; and the worship of the heavenly bodies, the sun, moon and stars, or of demons, angels, men and animals. Excessive attachment or veneration for anything, or that which borders on adoration."

6. **Sorcery**: "Magic; enchantment; witchcraft; divination by the assistance or supposed assistance of evil spirits, or the power of commanding evil spirits."

7. **Hatred**: "Great dislike or aversion; hate; enmity. Hatred is an aversion to evil, and may spring from utter disapprobation, as the hatred of vice or meanness; or it may spring from offenses or injuries done by fellow men, or from envy or jealousy, in which case it is usually accompanied with malevolence or malignity. Extreme hatred is abhorrence or detestation."

8. **Contention**: "Strife; struggle; a violent effort to obtain something, or to resist a person, claim or injury; contest; quarrel. Strife in words or debate; quarrel; angry contest; controversy."

9. **Jealousy**: "That passion or peculiar uneasiness which arises from the fear that a rival may rob us of the affection of one whom we love, or the suspicion that he has already done it; or it is the uneasiness which arises from the fear that another does or will enjoy some advantage which we desire for ourselves."

10. **Outbursts of Wrath**: "Violent anger; vehement exasperation; indignation."

11. **Selfish**: "Regarding one's own interest chiefly or solely; influenced in actions by a view to private advantage."

12. **Dissension**: "Disagreement in opinion, usually a disagreement which is violent, producing warm debates or angry words; contention in words; strife; discord; quarrel; breach of friendship and union."

13. **Heresy**: "A fundamental error in religion, or an error of opinion respecting some fundamental doctrine of religion. But in countries where there is an established church, an opinion is deemed heresy, when it differs from that of the church. The Scriptures being the standard of faith, any opinion that is repugnant to its doctrines, is heresy; but as men differ in the interpretation of Scripture, an opinion deemed heretical by one body of Christians, may be deemed orthodox by another."

14. **Envy**: "To feel uneasiness, mortification or discontent, at the sight of superior excellence, reputation or happiness enjoyed by another; to repine at another's prosperity; to fret or grieve one's self at the real or supposed superiority of another, and to hate him on that account."

15. **Murder**: "The act of unlawfully killing a human being with premeditated malice, by a person of sound mind. To constitute murder in law, the person killing another must be of sound mind or in possession of his reason, and the act must be done with malice pretense, afore-thought or premeditated; but malice may be implied, as well as express."

16. **Drunkenness**: "A state in which a person is overwhelmed or overpowered with spirituous liquors, so that his reason is; disordered, and he reels or staggers in walking. Drunkenness renders some persons stupid, others gay, others sullen, others furious."

17. **Revelry**: "Noisy festivity; clamorous jollity."

18. **Anything Else** that is similar to these.

Paul states that these characteristics of the flesh are to be eliminated through death of the flesh, which is the carnal nature. "Those who are Christ's have crucified the flesh with its passions and desires" (Gal. 5:24). We have become His own, and it is time to live in the Spirit! You may be tempted to live in the carnal nature, but you must live from your spirit man. That man is deep within you. Your spirit man is the real you.

One thing I have noticed among people as I talk with them is this understanding—the hardest part of our walk is the act of crucifying the flesh. The word *crucify* is very strong. Have you noticed that most people are aggressive in areas that deal with things we both want and need? We will compete for almost anything and be very forceful about it. But when it comes to treating our body as an enemy when it acts up, it seems to be out of the question for us to take authority over our body. We suddenly become very passive. The body you live in does not want you to rule over it. The body has a voice that sometimes is louder than our heart. We will have to discipline our bodies to live and walk in the Spirit.

> *If we live in the Spirit, let us also walk in the Spirit* (Galatians 5:25).

The Fruit of the Holy Spirit Through Our Spirit

Here is how Noah Webster defined the terms Paul used to describe the fruit of the spirit (also from the 1828 edition of his dictionary).

1. **Love:** "The love of God is the first duty of man, and this springs from just views of his attributes or excellencies of character, which afford the highest delight to the sanctified heart. Esteem and reverence constitute

ingredients in this affection, and a fear of offending him is its inseparable effect."

2. **Joy**: "The passion or emotion excited by the acquisition or expectation of good; that excitement of pleasurable feelings which is caused by success, good fortune, the gratification of desire or some good possessed, or by a rational prospect of possessing what we love or desire; gladness; exultation; exhilaration of spirits."

3. **Peace**: "In a general sense, a state of quiet or tranquility; freedom from disturbance or agitation; applicable to society, to individuals, or to the temper of the mind. Freedom from war with a foreign nation; public quiet. Freedom from internal commotion or civil war."

4. **Longsuffering**: "Bearing injuries or provocation for a long time; patient; not easily provoked. The Lord God, merciful and gracious, long-suffering and abundant in goodness."

5. **Kindness**: "Good will; benevolence; that temper or disposition which delights in contributing to the happiness of others, which is exercised cheerfully in gratifying their wishes, supplying their wants or alleviating their distresses; benignity of nature. Kindness ever accompanies love."

6. **Goodness**: "The state of being good; the physical qualities which constitute value, excellence or perfection; as the goodness of timber; the goodness of a soil. The moral qualities, which constitute Christian excellence; moral virtue; religion."

7. **Faithfulness**: "Fidelity; loyalty; firm adherence to allegiance and duty; as the faithfulness of a subject. Truth; veracity; as the faithfulness of God. Strict adherence to injunctions, and to the duties of a station; as the faithfulness of servants or ministers. Strict performance of promises, vows or covenants; constancy in affection; as the faithfulness of a husband or wife."

8. **Gentleness**: "Softness of manners; mildness of temper; sweetness of disposition; meekness."

9. **Control**: "To keep under check by a counter-register or double account. To check; to restrain; to govern."

You Are in the Spirit

The whole idea about walking in the Spirit is the yielding of your will to the Word of God as well as the Spirit of God. We are actually joined as in marriage. The apostle Paul said to the Romans:

> But when the Spirit of Christ empowers your life, you are not dominated by the flesh but by the Spirit. And if you are not joined to the Spirit of the Anointed One, you are not of him. Now Christ lives his life in you! And even though your body may be dead because of the effects of sin, his life-giving Spirit imparts life to you because you are fully accepted by God. Yes, God raised Jesus to life! And since God's Spirit of Resurrection lives in you, he will also raise your dying body to life by the same Spirit that breathes life into you! (Romans 8:9-11 TPT)

The power of the Holy Spirit that resurrects your dying body will also breathe life into you right now. Walking in the Spirit is possible even if it does not seem to be a reality at the moment. God would not have told us to do something that is not possible. He is also so very gracious to help you as well.

There are keys to remember when the flesh wants your spirit man to listen to it and yield to the point of manifesting its works. First, you must remind yourself that the Father God loves you and has amazing plans for you. Second, you must understand that when you seek God diligently, He rewards you. Part of that reward is answering your prayers! The Book of Hebrews tells us, "But without faith it is impossible to please Him, for he who comes to God must believe that He is, and that He is a rewarder of those who diligently seek Him" (Heb. 11:6).

I use these keys when my flesh and soul want to take over. I have pleased the Lord every time that I have chosen to walk in His Spirit. You will soon be encountering the victory over the flesh and soul when you implement these truths. He is asking you to be humble so that He can dwell with you and revive you! The Lord is strong and mighty. He wants you to know how much He Loves you!

> *For thus says the High and Lofty One who inhabits eternity, whose name is Holy: "I dwell in the high and holy place, with him who has a contrite and humble spirit, to revive the spirit of the humble, and to revive the heart of the contrite ones"* (Isaiah 57:15).

Sonship Through the Spirit

We have learned that God is a Father to us. That means that we are His children. He longs for us to mature in the knowledge of Him. You are adopted and do not need to be dominated by fear any longer. If you allow the Spirit of God to speak to you right this moment, He will tell you that you are a child of the Most High God! You will be won over because you will only be moved by His desires and not your own.

> *The mature children of God are only those who are moved by the impulses of the Holy Spirit. And you did not receive the "spirit of religious duty," leading you back into the fear of never being good enough. But you have received the "Spirit of Full Acceptance," enfolding you into the family of God. And you will never feel orphaned, for as he rises up within us, our spirits join him in saying the words of tender affection, "Beloved Father!" For the Holy Spirit makes God's fatherhood real to us as he whispers into our innermost being, "You are God's beloved child!" And since we are his true children, we qualify to share all his treasures, for indeed, we are heirs of God himself. And since we are joined to Christ, we also inherit all that he is and all that he has. We will experience being co-glorified with him provided that we accept his sufferings as our own (Romans 8:14-17 TPT).*

We are glorified with Jesus and share in all His treasures. These treasures, which have been given to us by God the Father, are the things that will fulfill us eternally. We need a revelation of the love of the Father God as we walk in the Spirit and experience answers to our prayers. Jesus prayed for all of us who would believe. He asked the Father that we would be able to operate in the same glory and relationship that the Father and the Son possesses (see John 17:20-26).

Feeding Your Spirit

Do you know how desperately your spirit man needs to be fed? The Word of God is heavenly bread (see John 6:31-37). God told Moses and the children of Israel that they needed to:

> *Meditate in it day and night, that you may observe to do according to all that is written in it. For then you will make your way prosperous, and then you will have good success. Have I not commanded you? Be strong and of good courage; do not be afraid, nor be dismayed, for the Lord your God is with you wherever you go* (Joshua 1:8-9).

The Lord wants you to be planted in His Word. This will cause you to be prosperous. Part of that prosperity includes the ability to have your prayers answered. This is possible as you mature in Him. In the Book of Psalms, King David talks about becoming a person who is steadfast in his or her stand in the Word. David spent a lot of time mediating on God's Word. He became a bold and fierce warrior for God's purposes.

> *Blessed is the man who walks not in the counsel of the ungodly, nor stands in the path of sinners, nor sits in the seat of the scornful; but his delight is in the law of the Lord, and in His law he* **meditates day and night. He shall be like a tree planted by the rivers of water,** *that brings forth its fruit in its season, whose leaf also shall not wither; and whatever he does shall prosper* (Psalm 1:1-3).

The Soul of Man

So many people want to know what the difference is between the spirit of man and soul of man. Discerning the truth about the difference between our spirit and our soul can be complicated because the Word of God, as a sword, is the only way to separate the two. I used to listen to my soul, thinking it was my spirit talking. What the Holy Spirit is speaking through your own human spirit may be entirely different than what your soul is speaking.

However, the soul, which includes your mind, your will, and your emotions, may be the predominant voice inside of you. The soul has the ability to imitate the voice of the Holy Spirit in your own human spirit. Also, evil spirits, called specifically "familiar spirits," will begin to guide you into error. The whole time, you may think that it is the voice of God.

The book of Hebrews explains it this way, "For the word of God is quick, and powerful, and sharper than any twoedged sword, piercing even to the dividing asunder of soul and spirit" (Heb. 4:12 KJV). It appears that the Word of God is the only thing that can separate and divide between the soul and the spirit of man. According to Scripture, the Word has to be sharp, quick, and powerful in order to accomplish a division between one's soul and one's spirit.

This shows us the extreme complexity in which we were created. Without the sword of the Spirit, which is the Word of God, we cannot discern between the voice of the spirit and the voice of the soul. We know that there are three parts to man. The apostle Paul stated the three parts of man in a prayer to the Thessalonians: "I pray God your whole spirit and soul and body be preserved blameless" (1 Thess. 5:23 KJV).

There is a unique process that your soul needs to go through in order to prevent your soul from working against you as you seek to walk in the Spirit. The soul is not instantly saved like the spirit of man. It takes time to allow the truth that is in the Word to be implemented in the soul. You can speed up this process by humbly accepting the truth. As it begins to change the way you think, you will see you soul becoming more like Jesus. Your soul will not resist your spirit, where the Holy Spirit dwells. The apostle James says, "Therefore lay aside all filthiness and overflow of wickedness, and receive with meekness the implanted word, which is able to save your souls" (James 1:21).

The apostle Paul also mentions the fact that the mind can be renewed. This is talking about the same process concerning the saving of the soul. "And be not conformed to this world: but be ye transformed by the renewing of your mind, that ye may prove what is that good, and acceptable, and perfect, will of God" (Rom. 12:2 KJV).

This is profound truth that Paul is relaying to us. When your mind is renewed, you are able to prove what God's will is for your life. A renewed mind gives a person freedom from worry about asking for the wrong things in prayer. A renewed mind will side with your spirit man and ask God for those things that He already intends to give you. It is a wonderful place to be, knowing the "good, and acceptable, and perfect, will of God." King David wrote about God restoring his soul. I know, as you are visited in prayer with His presence, you will experience this restoration. God wants all of you to be restored and in agreement with His perfect plan for you. You are so precious to Him.

The Body of Man

The truths about how God considers the action of your authority over your body are very important. First, the apostle Paul dealt with the body in a very strong manner. He told his readers in a letter to the Corinthians that they must discipline the body.

> Do you not know that those who run in a race all run, but one receives the prize? Run in such a way that you may obtain it. And everyone who competes for the prize is temperate in all things. Now they do it to obtain a perishable

crown, but we for an imperishable crown. Therefore I run thus: not with uncertainty. Thus I fight: not as one who beats the air. **But I discipline my body and bring it into subjection, lest, when I have preached to others, I myself should become disqualified** (1 Corinthians 9:24-27).

The body, therefore, will not automatically do what is right. The human body will need to be disciplined and given boundaries in order to function righteously. When the body is disciplined and the soul is renewed, they will be compatible with your spirit and the Holy Spirit's will. Second, the harmony with the Spirit of God comes as you submit your body to discipline. Your body will come into agreement with what is written about you in your books in Heaven.

Last, your body needs to be continually presented as a sacrifice to God in worship. This is done as your expected service to God, performed by everyone. "I beseech you therefore, brethren, by the mercies of God, that ye present your bodies a *living sacrifice*, holy, acceptable unto God, which is your *reasonable service*" (Rom. 12:1 KJV).

Meditate continually on these truths and the Lord will make sure you are in harmony with Heaven concerning your purpose and destiny. Remember that your spirit is alive because Christ dwells with you. Your mind knows and understands the will of God because you renew it with the Word of God. Your body manifests the righteous and holy ways of God because you subject it to discipline and bring it into submission. Heaven is going to answer you when you call because of your harmony with Heaven.

Chapter 10

PRAY IN THE SPIRIT

I thank God that I speak in tongues more than any of you.
—1 CORINTHIANS 14:18 NLT

When I had the experience of being with Jesus for forty-five minutes in 1992, one of the most important subjects that Jesus spoke of was praying in the Spirit. Praying in the Spirit involves the yielding of your tongue to the utterance of the Holy Spirit with your spirit. God will allow you to speak mysteries from the depths of God's heart through the depths of your spirit. This activity is for your private fellowship with God. When you are in a public assembly, the gift of prophecy is more effective in building everyone up than speaking in tongues unless someone has the gift of interpretation. People must be able to understand what is being said or it is of no value to others. The apostle Paul said:

> *For if you have the ability to speak in tongues, you will be talking only to God, since people won't be able to understand*

*you. You will be speaking by the power of the Spirit, but it will all be mysterious. But one who prophesies strengthens others, encourages them, and comforts them. **A person who speaks in tongues is strengthened personally, but one who speaks a word of prophecy strengthens the entire church**. I wish you could all speak in tongues, but even more I wish you could all prophesy. For prophecy is greater than speaking in tongues, unless someone interprets what you are saying so that the whole church will be strengthened* (1 Corinthians 14:2-5 NLT).

Jesus taught me that this was the single most important activity you could engage in that would open the door to the supernatural. That is why I must discuss it often in my teaching sessions. There exists the ability to both speak in tongues and interpret them as the Spirit wills. Yielding to the gift of prophecy and speaking the mysteries of God can be performed in your own, known language.

Remember that this activity is the way to engage the Holy Spirit in such a way that you can utter perfect prayers to the heavenly Father. Paul told the Corinthians:

That is what the Scriptures mean when they say, "No eye has seen, no ear has heard, and no mind has imagined what God has prepared for those who love him." But it was to us that God revealed these things by his Spirit. For his Spirit searches out everything and shows us God's deep secrets. No one can know a person's thoughts except that person's own spirit, and no one can know God's thoughts except God's own Spirit. And we have received God's Spirit (not the world's spirit), so we can know the wonderful things God has freely given us. When we tell you these things, we do not use words that come from human wisdom. Instead, we speak words given to us by the Spirit, using the Spirit's words to explain spiritual truths. But people who aren't spiritual can't receive these truths from God's Spirit. It all sounds foolish to them and they can't understand it, for only those who are spiritual can understand what the Spirit means (1 Corinthians 2:8-14 NLT).

Praying out of Weakness

I want you to know that when you pray in the Spirit out of your own inability to comprehend and perform, you are in a good position for the Holy Spirit to step in and accomplish God's will on your behalf. We do not always know the best way to pray. When you are going through a trial, you need understanding so that you can stand firm in your faith. God has given us help through the wonderful Holy Spirit. He will help you when you feel weak. He only wants the Father God's best for you. This is what the apostle Paul said.

*And the Holy Spirit helps us in our weakness. For example, we don't know what God wants us to pray for. But the Holy Spirit prays for us with groanings that cannot be expressed in words. And the Father who knows all hearts knows what the Spirit is saying, **for the Spirit pleads for us believers in harmony with God's own will**. And we know that God causes everything to work together for the good of those who love God and are called according to his purpose for them* (Romans 8:26-28 NLT).

I have found that when I yield to the Spirit of God in my weakness, He prays out the mysteries of God. The end result is that the will of God is done and everything always works out for my good. God has truly given us a powerful advocate to help us to pray more effectively.

Holiness

One of the benefits of yielding to the Holy Spirit in prayer is obtaining the environment of holiness that the Holy Spirit brings to your prayer life.

Praying in the most holy of faith (see Jude 20) will become your position as you let Him take you into Holy prayer. You must be holy as He is Holy (see 1 Peter 1:16). Every person who is born of the Spirit must live his or her life separated from the world. The apostle Paul was dealing with carnality within Christians at the Corinthian church. He told them:

> Therefore "Come out from among them and be separate, says the Lord. Do not touch what is unclean, and I will receive you. I will be a Father to you, and you shall be My sons and daughters, says the Lord Almighty" (2 Corinthians 6:17-18).

There has to be a separation between you and the world. This is because you are part of God's Kingdom and those of the world are part of satan's kingdom. Do not cause God to lose His distinction of being the High and Mighty One to the world because you did not live a separate life. We want the world to see Jesus through us. Even Moses wanted God to preserve His fame among the nations.

> And Moses said to the Lord: "Then the Egyptians will hear it, for by Your might You brought these people up from among them, and they will tell it to the inhabitants of this land. They have heard that You, Lord, are among these people; that You, Lord, are seen face to face and Your cloud stands above them, and You go before them in a pillar of cloud by day and in a pillar of fire by night. **Now if You kill these people as one man, then the nations which have heard**

of Your fame will speak, saying, '*Because the Lord was not able to bring this people to the land which He swore to give them, therefore He killed them in the wilderness.' And now, I pray, let the power of my Lord be great, just as You have spoken, saying,* '*The Lord is longsuffering and abundant in mercy, forgiving iniquity and transgression; but He by no means clears the guilty, visiting the iniquity of the fathers on the children to the third and fourth generation.' Pardon the iniquity of this people, I pray, according to the greatness of Your mercy, just as You have forgiven this people, from Egypt even until now*" (Numbers 14:13-19).

The Lord wants to preserve His heritage on the earth. Because you are His child, you will also be involved in the preservation of His heritage on the earth. You will inherit everything that God has, including His good name. So remember, God is Holy and so are you because you are a member of the family of God. He is deserving of our worship as a Holy God. "How great is the Lord, how deserving of praise, in the city of our God, which sits on His holy mountain!" (Ps. 48:1 NLT).

Sword of the Spirit

What many believers do not understand is that the Spirit of God is also represented as a sword. This sword is also referred to as the Word of God. We are instructed to pray always with all kinds of prayer and all types of prayer, but we are never to forget that the Spirit is also the Word of God represented as a sword.

*And take the helmet of salvation, and **the sword of the Spirit, which is the word of God; praying always** with all prayer and supplication in the Spirit, being watchful to* *this end with all perseverance and supplication for all the saints* (Ephesians 6:17-18).

As you are praying in the Spirit, be aware that you are praying with a sword. According to the previous verse, both the Word of God and the sword of the Spirit are synonymous with prayer. When you are in the Spirit praying, a sword is being used. It is your offensive weapon to use against any enemy. The enemy is threatened because of this weapon. You are very intimidating to the enemy when you show up for battle with the Word of God drawn and speaking under the influence of the Spirit.

I have been shown the effects of praying in the Spirit when I had my heavenly visitation in 1992. Jesus showed me that my prayers were very powerful and very effective.

Intercession

As you yield to the Holy Spirit, be firmly convinced that you are entering into your destiny. The Holy Spirit will quickly be moved into your destiny, and you may not even feel anything while you pray. That is because the Holy Spirit is interceding deep mysteries that do not go through your mind as they are uttered. The mind is bypassed because the things of the Spirit are spiritually discerned (see 1 Cor. 2:14).

The Spirit of God knows how to search your heart. He will retrieve all that is in your heart and express it to the Father God. He knows the will of God and will implement it if you will let Him. He is praying perfect prayers for you as you begin to utter in the Spirit. These prayers involve the things that are within your heart. You will always get what you pray for in the Spirit when you pray in this manner.

Now He who searches the hearts knows what the mind of the Spirit is, because He makes intercession for the saints according to the will of God (Romans 8:27).

Praying in the Spirit will bring you into what God called you to do. Just stay in His perfect will, allowing your purpose to be revealed. He prepared you to be conformed into the image of His Son. All of this is working around you and in you for His greater purpose. The apostle Paul said:

And we know that all things work together for good to those who love God, to those who are the called according to His purpose. For whom He foreknew, He also predestined to be conformed to the image of His Son, that He might be the firstborn among many brethren. Moreover whom He predestined, these He also called; whom He called, these He also justified; and whom He justified, these He also glorified (Romans 8:28-30).

All things work out for those who are called concerning His purpose, so we will not be able to explain how everything just seems to work out for the good. We are encountering the Kingdom when we see things start to shift and favor starts to surround us. No one is able to explain why the favor keeps coming, but we know why. We know that favor continues to come forth when we are called according to His purpose. I know that with Him I will succeed, and so will you, my friend. You will succeed every single time you are faced with a challenge. A task of the Holy Spirit that we need to examine more closely is the Holy Spirit's intercession on our behalf.

The Holy Spirit is assisting us by interceding for us. We then can have understanding beyond our own capability as we yield and allow the Holy Spirit to move upon us in intercession for others. As the Spirit of God directs me, I find myself praying more for others than I do for myself.

Spiritual Discipline

There are many subjects to concentrate on concerning your prayer life. One of the most important subjects, but also one of the least discussed, is spiritual discipline. Spiritual discipline is very necessary in order for the purpose and destiny of God to be made manifest, especially in your prayer life. To some, the Word's spiritual guidance and discipline are not compatible. I do not agree with that concept. There are many biblical truths that prove that God is a God of order and discipline. We first have to receive revelation concerning God's role as a Father in our lives. Once we recognize God's role as a Father, we will arrive at the conclusion that we are His children as well. If we are committed to Him as children, then He also is committed to us as a Father God. His commitment to us also includes the Father God's discipline in our lives. The writer of Hebrews addresses this subject in detail:

> As you endure this divine discipline, remember that God is treating you as his own children. Who ever heard of a child who is never disciplined by its father? If God doesn't discipline you as he does all of his children, it means that you are illegitimate and are not really his children at all. Since we respected our earthly fathers who disciplined us, shouldn't we submit even more to the discipline of the Father of our spirits, and live forever? (Hebrews 12:7-9 NLT)

The Father will train you in prayer. In order to pray and enforce the covenant, you will have to use your God-given authority in Christ Jesus. Exercising that authority will take discipline and tenacity on our part. God is committed to revealing truth to you if you desire it. We will have to endure discipline so that we can participate in all that God is accomplishing in our lives. Let Him speak to you today as you encounter His visitation. All of your prayers will be answered. He will reveal Himself to you and visitation will occur as you yield to the ways of His Spirit. He is the "Father of all spirits." He is breathing on you now as you allow the Spirit to pray His perfect will for your life.

Persistence in Prayer

When you stay persistent in prayer, then angels will show up. You will have to learn to have tenacity to stay in the Spirit and not be denied. This is the very thing that Daniel had to do to obtain victory. Daniel received the answers to his prayers. But more importantly, God showed him how vital he was to God's plan in history. This revelation of God's plan to Daniel also included angel visitation!

> *Suddenly, a hand touched me, which made me tremble on my knees and on the palms of my hands. And he said to me, "O Daniel, man greatly beloved, understand the words that I speak to you, and stand upright, for I have now been sent to you." While he was speaking this word to me, I stood trembling. Then he said to me, "Do not fear, Daniel, for from the first day that you set your heart to understand, and to humble yourself before your God, your words were heard; and I have come because of your words. But the prince of the kingdom of Persia **withstood me twenty-one days**; and behold, Michael, one of the chief princes, came to help me, for I had been left alone there with the kings of Persia. Now I have come to make you understand what will happen to your people in the latter days, for the vision refers to many days yet to come" (Daniel 10:10-14).*

Whenever you yield to the Spirit of God in prayer, remember to be conscious that angels are being summoned to assist in the implementation of what is being spoken in tongues. You will have to place yourself in the shoes of Daniel as He sought God for His perfect will.

The ministry of angels is overtly returning into the believer's mind and ministry in the earth. We are rapidly approaching the end of an age. In a visitation, the Lord informed me of the coming acceleration of the intervention of angels at this time because we are lagging as believers in this stage of the end-time scenario. Jesus let me know so I can be aware of the situation and let others know of the increased ministry of angels at this moment in history. The angels are sent as ministers who are flames of fire (see Ps. 104:4).

The word for "flaming" here is the Hebrew word *lahat* (Strong's number H3857). It means to blaze or set on fire. The word is also used to describe the flaming sword that the guardian cherubim possessed. The cherubim guarded the way to the tree of life (see Gen. 3:24).

One of several of my angels is always with me when I am on assignment for God. One angel in particular loves to burn brightly for the Lord Jesus Christ. He is so bright, and he is quite fast. If you are ever around me when he comes in, you are in for a real encounter. He burns so holy and bright that I immediately catch on fire. Then, as a result of his arrival, the Holy Spirit starts to minister to people all around me as they begin to experience the same flames of fire.

Persistence in prayer will also draw the attention of the enemy. He will do everything within his power prevent your prayers and to cause you to stop. The enemy's desire to be a hindrance to your prayers is also why angels are assigned to you. They have been given special orders concerning you in order to protect you from any harm or opposition. The psalmist wrote about this when he said, "For he will order his angels to protect you wherever you go" (Ps. 91:11 NLT). Because you are in the secret place of the Most High and make Him your dwelling place, you qualify for this help (see Ps. 91:9).

Remember to speak the Word of the Lord in prayer. The angels harken unto the voice of God. This is part of praying in the spirit. You can proclaim the Word of the Lord in prayer in tongues or prophesy as the Spirit wills. Sometimes, I even have gotten the interpretation of my tongues as I pray in the Spirit. I have been mindful at times that, according to the apostle Paul, I may even be speaking a tongue that the angels understand (see 1 Cor. 13:1).

Be assured that your encounters with our loving heavenly Father will cause you to understand that discipline provides more productive results because it helps us to maintain a steadfastness in our prayer and visitation times. This is where you will have to refuse to move, and you will have to be established in the perfect will of God according to His Word. Angels will then arrive to do the Lord's will on your behalf. Angels love to please God. It brings them great joy to perform His Word for you during prayer.

> Bless the Lord, you His angels, who excel in strength, who
> do His word, heeding the voice of His word. Bless the Lord,
> all you His hosts, you ministers of His, who do His pleasure.
> Bless the Lord, all His works, in all places of His dominion.
> Bless the Lord, O my soul! (Psalm 103:20-22)

Waiting on God

The fellowship of the Holy Spirit will often challenge your patience during the times of praying in the Spirit. Your mind and body will feel left out of this activity, so they will start to try to dominate the situation. When this happens, you will know that your mind and body are acting as a spoiled child who wants your attention. You must be patient to wait on the Lord. You must put to death the misdeeds of the body and bring into captivity every thought of your mind. If you want to be able to pray in the Spirit more than ten minutes without getting pushed out of your prayer and visitation time by the enemy, then you must be mindful of the following two Scripture references.

Concerning the Body

For if you live according to the flesh you will die; but if by the Spirit you put to death the deeds of the body, you will live. For as many as are led by the Spirit of God, these are sons of God (Romans 8:13-14).

Concerning the Mind

For the weapons of our warfare are not carnal but mighty in God for pulling down strongholds, casting down arguments and every high thing that exalts itself against the knowledge of God, bringing every thought into captivity to the obedience of Christ, and being ready to punish all disobedience when your obedience is fulfilled (2 Corinthians 10:4-6).

The truths in these scriptures have advanced my prayer and visitation time to well over that ten-minute mark. Now, my goal is to compete with the apostle Paul. He is the one who spoke this statement, "I thank my God I speak with tongues more than you all" (1 Cor. 14:18). I started speaking in tongues at nineteen. I know I can beat Paul. Some of you have the same opportunity. Would it not be great to have Paul meet you in Heaven and be congratulated on exceeding him? I am sure that the apostle Paul would not mind if we surpassed him in speaking in tongues; he is well aware of the benefits of the activity of speaking in other tongues.

God Needs You

I would like to share with you a very amazing experience that I had. In the summer of 1986, I had already graduated in the spring with my bachelor's degree. I had been fasting on and off and praying continually for approximately three years, beginning in the second year of college and ending shortly after this experience. For that last year, I had been led to skip my dinner every day. There were times when I would pray in the Spirit, otherwise known as praying in tongues, so long and deeply that I could not transition back to English. I yielded to the Spirit in times of prayer for days at a time without eating a single meal during the summer months. I always missed dinner during the school year. After graduation, I took summer classes in the morning and spent the remaining time praying. This occurred for several hours a day on average. Most of this was done in the Spirit—praying in a heavenly language, which was not my own known language. I prayed out loud for hours without stopping.

The apostle Paul explains:

> *For if I pray in a tongue, my spirit prays, but my understanding is unfruitful. What is the conclusion then? I will pray with the spirit, and I will also pray with the understanding. I will sing with the spirit, and I will also sing with the understanding* (1 Corinthians 14:14-15).

One morning as I was finishing a session of prayer, I felt the Lord prompt me to sing to Him "Amazing Grace," which I knew very well. But it wasn't that easy. He asked me to sing it to Him in the Spirit, to sing in languages unknown to me, being led and inspired by the Spirit. My thinly walled dorm room was in a building that housed many students, and I knew that people would hear me. I did not feel quite comfortable with that situation, but I felt the Lord compelling me, so I did. I sang

"Amazing Grace" in tongues. Even though it was in a language that I did not know, its sound was beautiful and familiar. The anointing hit me with such power that I forgot about people hearing me. I sang, exerting my voice loudly as though in a concert hall. I am compelled to believe the Spirit sent my song forth as a prophecy.

Resolved that I had fulfilled the Lord's request, I relaxed into my next project. Almost immediately, a knock sounded at my door. I was concerned because I had been singing loudly and I knew that I probably had disturbed someone. I opened my door slightly. A young man introduced himself to me. Through the cracked door, the young man explained that he was a missionary's son from the Yucatán Peninsula who had been sent to go to college in the same town as my college. He wanted to meet me because I was singing "Amazing Grace" in his dialect from the Yucatán Peninsula. He wanted to know what town I had grown up in because I had the same dialect as he did, which was rare. I looked at him in shock, and I wondered if he was joking. He was very serious and was crying. I knew he was serious. I told him that I knew no other language except English and that I had never been to the Yucatán Peninsula. He said, "That's impossible because you just sang 'Amazing Grace' in my dialect perfectly." He further explained that some of the words, which were more difficult, were pronounced very well.

At this point I asked him to come in because he was really crying and I thought that I needed to hear his whole story. He told me that he had grown up down in Central America and that his parents had felt he should go to Bible school for training. He was sent to a school in town about twenty minutes away from my college. He told me that while he was at this college, the Spirit of the Lord came upon him and he spoke in tongues with other languages, as was told in the Bible. The fact was that the college of that particular movement or denomination does not believe the Holy Spirit operates through speaking in tongues in this dispensation. He must have been reported to the authorities in his college because they had dismissed him from the college, citing doctrinal conflicts between his actions and the college's belief that the gift of speaking in tongues is not for today. He was heartbroken because he felt that he had let his parents down.

Rather than go back to the Yucatán, he had discovered that my college believed the Holy Spirit operated this way today. He had applied and was accepted into the college. He had just moved in across the hallway from me. He was praying and felt damaged by all that happened. He had just sat down when all of a sudden he heard "Amazing Grace" being sung in his native language. So when he came over to talk to me, he was excited because he felt God had given him a friend who was from the same exact region as he. But it was a far greater act of love from the Lord then he realized. Through this experience, God confirmed to him the authenticity of his walk with God and the present-day ministry of the Holy Spirit through the supernatural gift of tongues.

Ending the account here would be enough to encourage anyone. But it was only the beginning. For the next week, I saw him every day and I would sense the Holy Spirit wanting to speak out loud through me to him. So I began to yield to what God was doing. I spoke in the most fluent Spanish for days and he interpreted. I was amazed at how the Holy Spirit was covering specific events in the future, even names and places and events that had to take place but would not happen unless I prayed them out and gained a certain degree of understanding. This understanding developed within my spirit or inner man, went through my soul—which includes my mind, emotions, and will—and then proceeded outwardly through my body as I spoke in tongues.

In some cases, the Holy Spirit was revealing, in Spanish, that I was behind schedule on some events and that there were specific people waiting for me to arrive at their location. I realized that I was hindering progress, and that my failure affected other people! Through the process of this supernatural experience, I discovered the Holy Spirit telling me that I was to have been in Tulsa yesterday! So I called the bus station, and I got a ticket to go to Tulsa, Oklahoma. That morning at about three, the Spirit was also saying, in perfect Spanish, that I already had a job, car, place to stay, and would be attending a two-year training program at a local college for ministry preparation. The Holy Spirit even revealed the name of the college and its location. I knew of this college and had wanted to attend it. The supernatural thing about this situation was that this young missionary's son did not know any of the situation concerning my desire to attend that college in Tulsa. He was just translating what I was saying in my prayer language and telling me.

This missionary's son took me to the bus station that next morning. We said our goodbyes, and I took one of the last seats next to a young lady. The lady was attending her second year at the same college that the Spirit of God told me I was going to attend in the fall. She reassured me and offered to help in any way possible. When we got to Tulsa, she gave me a ride to Oral Roberts University where I felt I should go next. There I met a man who was a security guard for the campus. He happened to know where a friend of mine lived who was my hall counselor at the college from which I had just graduated. My counselor had graduated a year ago. The Lord was leading me every step of the way. When I arrived at his residence, His leading was obvious. It was as though God had sent him and his wife ahead to Tulsa, just for me. I knocked on the door with my luggage, and they answered. They were so helpful. They asked if I needed a place to live because they had a big house. I said, "Yes!" He then said that he had a position open at his company and offered me a job. I was working at my new job by five in the afternoon that very day. I was able to ride with him every day to work. I eventually got a car that was supernaturally paid in full by someone just for me. I attended the college for two years and graduated in 1987, just as the Spirit had spoken to me before I even went to Tulsa as the Lord had told me to do. He had spoken to me in a heavenly encounter that involved a foreign language that I was able to speak supernaturally.

I was deeply touched by the way the Lord reached out to this individual. God's ultimate goal in habitation is to help you to be a part of what He is doing on the earth in the lives of others. I was able to see this in action, and I still see it happen today. I want to also point out that as I obeyed the Lord, He not only used me to encourage another brother in Christ, but He also used my obedience as seed to meet my needs supernaturally so that I could fulfill God's destiny for my own life.

Our Goal

Our goal should be to pray into God's heavenly realm and to live in that realm also. To tell you the truth, I do not even pray for myself anymore. I find as I yield to the Spirit of God I am praying out mysteries. After praying in the spirit, all my prayers are answered. In fact, some of the prayers that I do not even pray are answered because God my Father is so good! There is visitation in prayer. I believe that if we will come to Him in spirit and in truth, we will have many testimonies about how the Spirit led us into answered prayer.

The veil from the flesh and this world has been taken off because you have turned toward the Lord. I believe it is your time to experience visitation and answered prayer in the freedom of the Holy Spirit.

> But whenever someone turns to the Lord, the veil is taken away. For the Lord is the Spirit, and wherever the Spirit of the Lord is, there is freedom. So all of us who have had that veil removed can see and reflect the glory of the Lord. And the Lord—who is the Spirit—makes us more and more like him as we are changed into his glorious image (2 Corinthians 3:16-18 NLT).

The Lord will establish you as you yield to Him. You are already established in Heaven, but praying in the Spirit will implement the heavenly realm for you into this earthly realm and establish God's perfect destiny in your life. Stay ready, as a good soldier for Jesus, and God will certainly come and visit you as you pray in the Spirit. The Lord is saying to you just as He did to Zerubbabel:

> *Moreover the word of the Lord came to me, saying: "The hands of Zerubbabel have laid the foundation of this temple; his hands shall also finish it. Then you will know"* (Zechariah 4:8-9).

Chapter 11

KNOWING HIS WAYS

Watching Sid's Supernatural Show

Once I was watching *It's Supernatural!* with Sid Roth, and there was a couple on his program. They were talking about praying and asking God to show them those for whom they were to do "acts of kindness." It grew into a big group of people who were doing things as the Spirit would lead them. As I watched the program, the Lord told me that I was to assemble three Thanksgiving meals with all the fixings and turkey and give them to my pastor at my church to hand out to three families that needed the supplies or they would not be able to have Thanksgiving. So I did what the Lord had impressed upon me to do, and the pastor gave them to the three families on Thanksgiving. The church usually did this every year, but they could not afford it this particular year, so they were touched, as well as the people who received the meals. I got a call telling me that the meals had been distributed and that it was touching to the families as well as to the staff at the church. I was overcome with the goodness of God. I hung up, and then the phone rang again. I had spent seventy-five dollars in total for the three meals. Not even thirty seconds had gone by, so when the phone rang again I thought it was the pastor. I thought he had forgotten to tell me something and was calling me back. I answered. It was a family member who was notifying us that we were inheriting seventy-five thousand dollars. They needed our information so they could transfer the money. So the Lord taught me that watching Sid Roth's *It's Supernatural!* program is one thing, but acting on what I hear and see on the show is a totally different activity. Such situations require that I put my faith into action.

Putting Heaven in a Corner

Jesus has taught me that there are things that we can do that will cause Heaven to have to act on behalf of others who cannot pay me back. He showed me that if we will do things for children, the angels that are with them, who always see the face of their Father in Heaven, will go and tell on me. Then I will be rewarded greatly for doing these things for a child. He also said that when you take care of the widow and the orphan, your actions cause Heaven to be required to act on your behalf when you feed the poor. God will have to repay you. He also showed me that when you do not deliver yourself in a situation, then Heaven is required to deliver you, and your next step will be a supernatural step.

They Will Not Let Me Bless Them

During my heavenly visitation in 1992, Jesus also showed me that there are Christians who will not let Him bless them. He walked up to someone who was standing near with us when I was in Heaven. The person became an example of what Jesus was explaining to me concerning those who will not allow Jesus to bless them. Jesus reached out and began to bless that particular individual. As He pronounced the blessing over them, substance came out of His hand, but it bounced back to us instead of going to them. He turned to me with tears and said, "You see, they will not let Me bless them."

Knowing His Ways

*He made known His **ways** to Moses, His **acts** to the children of Israel* (Psalm 103:7).

I have seen such a change in my life since Jesus, the Son of God, taught me about prayer. I remember all of the books and teachings I have encountered over my lifetime on the subject of prayer. What was most profound to me was the discrepancy between the person teaching and my own prayer life. I realized that something was missing from my prayer time, and I wanted it resolved quickly. Then, Jesus changed me on the inside. Now the way I pray is also changed forever. You see, in 1992 I had a near-death experience. In the fall of that year, that experience occurred, and it has imprinted on me the very personality of Jesus. (Please read my book *Heavenly Visitation* for the whole account.)

I learned the power of prayer in that visitation. I stood outside my body in the operating room and I waited for someone in Heaven to come and either take me to be with Jesus or send me back to my body. I could not get back myself, no matter how hard I tried. I encountered Jesus, the Messiah, in person. He taught me even as the doctor continued to operate on my physical body. Jesus announced that He was going to show me the effectiveness of the prayers of His children. He extended His arm and pointed. Instantly, as though the destination had come to us, we were standing on a mountaintop overlooking what appeared to be White Sands Missile Range in New Mexico. Jesus said to me, "Here is what happens when you begin to pray." A fireball resembling an atomic explosion erupted. As we watched, the plume created by the fireball towered high above us. Jesus then pointed out a shock wave that was traveling away from the explosion in every direction. The shock wave came quickly and with great intensity. It was so powerful that it removed everything standing in its path.

Jesus encouraged me to never give up on my prayers and to always pray with intensity and faith. Even when I did not see changes or immediate results, Jesus told me to continue praying and keep praying through until I knew my prayer was complete. He said, "You see, your prayers *are* effective; they *do* work." I realized that when we pray, a shock wave emanates from us that will level everything in its path. Anything hindering the answer will be pushed out of the way. The most profound thing about this was not the big, red fireball explosion that was going heavenward, which was very *spectacular*. Jesus said that the shockwave moving at a great speed and power along the ground was the power of the *supernatural,* and that it was effectively moving things out of my way. This supernatural power to overcome all obstacles occurs when I pray. We sometimes look for the spectacular and thereby completely miss the supernatural!

Jesus taught me that we are to be infused with the breath of Heaven, speaking God's words for God's purposes on the earth about those things that concern us. Jesus explained to me the incredible difference a person can make on earth when they live in their authority as a child of God. He said, "For example, your area of authority extends thirty feet around you. You have developed your spirit to have authority in that geographic area. People within that perimeter will be under your spiritual influence and will encounter the power and authority in which you walk. I have men on the earth who affect whole cities with their presence when they enter them." Jesus then showed me an apostle I knew. As I watched him enter a city, every devil knew the apostle was there. When the apostle spoke, the city responded because of his sphere of authority.

In the Book of Psalms, we see that Moses received revelation of God's *ways,* but the children of Israel received revelation in God's actions. This is so important to fully understand. This verse sums up what happened to me when I encountered Jesus in person. If you will let the Bible change you and help you to mature in the Spirit, then successful prayer is imminent.

The original Hebrew word used for "ways" is *derek* (Strong's number H1870), which means a "road (as trodden); figuratively, a course of life or mode of action." We must realize that God's *ways* involve a *course* or *mode of action.* Father God is the highest standard in the universe. The prophet Isaiah explained it this way, "For as the heavens are higher than the earth, so are My ways higher than your ways, and My thoughts than your thoughts" (Isa. 55:9).

On the other hand, the original Hebrew word for "acts," `aliylah` (Strong's number H5949), is the "sense of effecting; an exploit (of God), or a performance (of man, often in a bad sense); by implication, an opportunity." The point here is that you can observe God as a spectator as He performs wonderful acts, but you will never know Him intimately because you are only an observer. When you get to know Him by the Word of God and the Holy Spirit's revelation, you will then learn His ways.

> *Know His ways, not just His acts!*

*He revealed his **character** to Moses and his **deeds** to the people of Israel (Psalm 103:7 NLT).*

What does it mean to you when you are asked, "What are some of your best character traits?" To answer that question, you have to think about yourself in a positive way and also think quickly! Most of the time, we do not see ourselves the way God see us. Sometimes, we get so beaten down by the environment in which we live or in which we place ourselves, we must pause and really think about the question before we can answer.

The truth is that many times, because we do not think of ourselves the way we should, we have to run to a friend and ask them to assess our character qualities. We always seem to apologize about any deficiencies we think we may have, even if we do compliment ourselves. Those people with whom we feel comfortable are generally those who understand us. We also expect them to tell us the truth about everything because we trust them. It is not just about feeling comfortable; a truly good friend is going to be truthful. Truth is what sets us free. I know that the character of someone will teach me something about his or her ways. The truth will tell us how we are doing and show us the areas where we need to improve.

Our character has to be proven in the fires of life so that our first response under pressure is the correct response. How many of us have been insulted or been under so much pressure that we thought about what the right response should have been long after we walked away from the situation? I have found that, eventually, your character will become so rock solid that you will be able to do and say the right thing under pressure immediately. Moses spent time in very intimate situations with the Lord. Can you imagine how being with the Lord in "His environment" felt? He spent multiple forty-day visits with Him on the mountain. It says that he received the law through angels on Mt. Sinai (see Gal. 3:19). So God's environment is full of glorious things to which we may not be accustomed. His heavenly entourage was there with Moses as well.

My wife and I once spent four days on the road with our spiritual parents, Jesse and Cathy Duplantis. I cannot put into words everything that we received during that time. It changed everything about us. One of the long-term effects of this was our character. You see, what I may have observed from a distance about Brother Jesse and Sister Cathy are just their acts or deeds. When we spent time with them, our ways of doing things changed and our character was affected. People started commenting to me and to Jesse about what they noticed. We have started to walk in that which Jesse and Cathy are walking. That is what was meant by Psalm 103:7. Israel observed the acts and deeds of their God delivering them out of Egypt. But when it came time to accept the invitation to go up the mountain and fellowship with Him, they refused to enter in.

Moses, however, did go up and was taught for many days. At the end of these intensely glorious meetings, Moses had glorious beams coming out of face and had to veil himself because he began to look like the One with whom He spent time. He also understood God's direction based on the revelation of God's character to him. He finally realized that there was much more about God than he previously realized. This led him to ask for more because God was holding back something. God held back His glory that flowed from His face. God could not permit it because He knew that seeing His face with all that glory would be the end of Moses's body—it would be too much for him. God needed him to stay alive for his destiny and purpose.

What is amazing is that even the back parts of God caused Moses's face to shine. The children of Israel began to cry out in fear and have Moses cover his face for them. Why did it not produce any fear in Moses concerning God's glory and His face? Not only was Moses not afraid, but also he asked for so much that God had to coach him and tell him, "You're about to kill yourself with your request, and I cannot allow you to do it!" Moses lost fear because he knew God's ways; he did not just know God's acts. Before you pray, spend time with Him on the mountain. Let Him permeate you with His glory. Then, from that place of fellowship and communion, pray and you will see that your prayers will be answered.

Understanding your need to spend time with the Lord is so important for the rest of your life. The forty-five minutes that I spent with Jesus caused an impartation that infused me with His ways and character. It infused me with far more than His acts. I became more like Him inside. It is *who He is, not just what He does!* Now when I pray, I already know that He is ready to answer. I know that He is always ready to respond because I know that He wants to provide His will for my life to me. Out of love for me He gives, not just out of obligation. Jesus said in John 15, in reference to the vine and the branches, "If you abide in Me, and My words abide in you, you will ask what you *desire*, and it shall be done for you" (John 15:7).

> *Fellowship is communication, dialogue, and sharing intimate secrets. It should not be done because it is required, but because it is your passion. The Lord wants to have fellowship with you. It is not a requirement on His part. It is His passion. You can let Him in because He is good. He is faithful. He is truthful; He is a friend who sticks closer than a brother.*

Chapter 12

VISITATION IN PRAYER

Thou hast granted me life and favour, and thy visitation
hath preserved my spirit. —Job 10:12 KJV

Most of us know the story of Job and what he endured. When you read what Job stated in Job 10:12, you realize the depth of Job's trust in the Lord. We all have our stories about the challenging experiences in our lives that we had to endure to completion. One of the most precious things that can happen to us in these hard times is the visitation of the Lord in our time of travail. Your relationship with the Almighty God proceeds to a new and a higher level when He comes in and grants you life when there is death all around you. He grants you favor when you have fallen out of favor. The Almighty will consistently protect us and bring us completely through hardship. He wants you whole, so He begins to reveal Himself to you as a way of healing you.

There are certain attributes of God Almighty that He wants to reveal to you. You might think you are going in to pray in the secret place, but He has other plans. He wants to visit with you and heal you. He wants to grant you life and favor through visitation. Let us look at what King David wrote. The Almighty God revealed His character to David. David therefore became aware that those who put their trust in Him *are abundantly satisfied.*

> *Your mercy, O Lord, is in the heavens; Your faithfulness reaches to the clouds. Your righteousness is like the great mountains; Your judgments are a great deep; O Lord, You preserve man and beast. How precious is Your lovingkindness, O God! Therefore the children of men put their trust under the shadow of Your wings. They are **abundantly satisfied** with the fullness of Your house, and You give them drink from the river of Your pleasures. For with You is the fountain of life; in Your light we see light. Oh, continue Your lovingkindness to those who know You, and Your righteousness to the upright in heart* (Psalm 36:5-10).

Here, King David is expressing a time of visitation before the Ark, in the House of the Lord. He describes the Mercy Seat and the wings of the cherubim that cover the Ark. These portions of David's writings show the benefits of having visitation with God in the secret place of His presence.

The Benefits of Visitation

Mercy

> *Your mercy-seat love is limitless, reaching higher than the highest heavens* (Psalm 36:5 TPT).

When we pray, we should have an eager expectation that has God heard us. He is rich in mercy and will answer our prayers. It is always important to remember His mercy and His response to prayer is guaranteed when you approach God in prayer. As His Spirit engulfs us, revelation begins to come forth and we realize how wonderful He is. We long to know Him, and He longs to be known by us. God Almighty wants to have fellowship with us. He is so rich in mercy that by revelation, He shows us how His love for us is without limit. You cannot find a place that is too high that His mercy is not present. He will have mercy on you as you visit with Him and adore Him.

> *During visitation, the Almighty whispers, "I long to answer your prayers. I will, after I unveil My mercy to you."*

Faithfulness

> *Your great faithfulness is so infinite, stretching over the whole earth* (Psalm 36:5 TPT).

As we sit in His presence, saturated by His love for us, we begin to realize that we have allowed this earthly realm to have preeminence in our lives and that, instead, His *heavenly reality realm* should have preeminence. It is good to be before Him, beholding His faithfulness as He covers you.

God has revealed Himself faithful in nature. He is even faithful to the birds who do not sow or reap but are not lacking anything because He feeds them (see Matt. 6:26). When God speaks, you can be sure that He will do that very thing. His Word will not come back to Him void, but will accomplish its intent and prosper (see Isa. 55:11).

You see, He cannot and will not go back on His Word. That is why it is so important to know what He said. It is not God's character to go against what He has already proclaimed, so concentrate on what He says and His faithfulness will bring it to pass!

> *During visitation, the Almighty whispers, "I long to answer your prayers. I will, after I unveil My faithfulness to you."*

Righteousness

> *Your righteousness is unmovable, just like the mighty mountains* (Psalm 36:6 TPT).

Righteousness is in the foundation of His throne (see Ps. 89:14). That means that everything is in right standing with Him in Heaven. His whole Kingdom is based on being right! That means that you can trust Him to do the right thing for you in your situation. So do not have any care about the situation you are facing. "Commit your way to the Lord, trust also in Him, and He shall bring it to pass. He shall bring forth your *righteousness as the light*, and your justice as the noonday" (Ps. 37:5-6).

His righteousness is immovable and always a foundation for whatever the Lord does or says. He desires you to be right in the middle of the way of righteousness. Abiding where He lives is my heart's desire, always. It is important for each of us to have a heart's desire to abide with Him always.

> *During visitation, the Almighty whispers, "I long to answer your prayers. I will, after I unveil My righteousness to you."*

Just Judgments

> *Your judgments are as full of wisdom as the oceans are full of water* (Psalm 36:6 TPT).

As you wait in His presence, you will see, as you have never seen before, that you are in the good hand of the Just Judge. Not only will He do things right on your behalf, but He will bring justice where justice is required. There may be discrepancies between what is written about you in Heaven and what the enemy has brought into your situation. The enemy will craft blatant lies against you and against God to try to prevent your victory in any situation. Just judgments come to correct these discrepancies and force the enemy out. Justice comes and fills your environment. Justice then rules out the enemy's deceptive tactics. The Almighty God is infinite in wisdom. He wants to rule over whatever comes against you. Visitation in prayer connects you to the truth in the heavenly realm. It allows you yield to what the books in Heaven say is the truth about the circumstances. Justice comes as the angels begin to implement the heavenly plan into your life so that true justice can be brought to the situation.

> *During visitation, the Almighty whispers, "I want to answer your prayers. I will, after I unveil My just judgements to you."*

Kindness

> *Your tender care and kindness leave no one forgotten, not a man nor even a mouse* (Psalm 36:6 TPT).

The Lord watches over all those who are His own. He even watches over the stranger (see Ps. 146:9). Jesus is the kindest person I know. He is always thinking of how He can get people to believe and participate in His provision in every area. He will do things for people because He wants them to prosper in every area of their lives. However, we must move into faith or we will not please Him (see Heb. 11:6). He will not forget you. Just accept this character trait with God. He will be there to help you. He desires that you will be healed of any hurt that you may have experienced concerning rejection and abandonment. God did not do any of those things against you. You must allow the Holy Spirit to heal you. You must move into faith so that God will visit you mightily when you pray.

> *During visitation, the Almighty whispers, "I want to answer your prayers. I will, after I unveil My kindness to you and heal you."*

Love

> O God, how extravagant is your cherishing love! (Psalm 36:7 TPT)

God has so much more goodness and mercy in Him then we could ever comprehend. He will reveal Himself to us forever. We will not come to the point where we fully understand His gracious and giving heart. He really does adore us beyond our imagination. He has a passion to bless us beyond what we could ever possibly comprehend. When I have met with Jesus over the years, I am always in awe of how much He loves me. Jesus does not just "love us," He *is* Love. Once He reveals Himself to you, you start to understand that He is love. He wants you to know how much He cherishes you. Healing comes after this revelation of His great love. Jesus is love because that is who He happens to be; He is not love because of what He does.

> *During visitation, the Almighty whispers, "I want to answer your prayer. I will, after I unveil My extravagant love to you."*

A Hiding Place

*All mankind can find a hiding place under the shadow of
your wings* (Psalm 36:7 TPT).

Any time you see phrases referring to God's wings, they are referring to the Holy of Holies. He is indicating that it is time to place
yourself before the Ark of the Covenant. Usually, King David and
Moses talk about placing yourself before the Ark because that is what
King David and Moses actually experienced. The hiding place had to
do with the shadow of the Almighty. The shadow was formed because
of the wings of the cherubim who were on the Mercy Seat and whose
wings covered that Mercy Seat. They are referred to a number of times
in God's Word. The wings of the cherubim on the Mercy Seat represent
protection for you that exceeds your comprehension.

The key to this is allowing the Holy Spirit, through revelation, to
make the Most High your dwelling place and stay "in the shadow of His
wings." If God gives you understanding of this concept, then you will
stay in close proximity to the cherubim that cover Him because you are
aware that place is where the Most High dwells. Moses said, "Because
you have made the Lord, who is my refuge, even the Most High, your
dwelling place, no evil shall befall you" (Ps. 91:9-10).

> *During visitation, the Almighty whispers, "I want to answer
> your prayers. I will, after I unveil My **hiding place** to you."*

Anointing

*All may drink of the anointing from the abundance of your
house!* (Psalm 36:8 TPT)

I long to have everything that God has for me. One thing we know
about the Almighty is that He is rich. His abundance will supply any

need. There is an anointing that comes from His abundance. His supply will provide for every longing in you. He wants you to drink of the anointing and be full of His goodness. You will find that out of His spiritual abundance you will be satisfied when you drink deeply of Him. Your prayers will be answered as you sit in His House and drink of His goodness. Prayers will be answered in time. You can go and drink of Him, for now you know that He is good.

Any bondage that you may have encountered shall be broken because of the anointing oil. "It shall come to pass in that day that his burden will be taken away from your shoulder, and his yoke from your neck, and the yoke will be destroyed because of *the anointing oil*" (Isa. 10:27).

The anointing oil will set you apart as you are saturated with the Holy One. The Holy Spirit is the epitome of truth and will lead you into the deep things of God through revelation. "But you have an anointing from the *Holy One, and you know all things*" (1 John 2:20). The teacher resides in you, and He wants to help you receive what He has for you to receive. As you drink of His anointing, the teacher will teach you all things that are true. Drink deeply and allow the truth to saturate your spirit as you abide in Him and the anointing oil abides in you. John said in His letter to believers:

> But the anointing which **you have received** from Him **abides in you**, and you do not need that anyone teach you; but as the same anointing teaches you concerning all things, and is true, and is not a lie, and just as it has taught you, you will **abide in Him** (1 John 2:27).

The power of your prayer life is ignited when you drink from the holy anointing. When the holy anointing is present in your prayers, bondages are broken, knowledge of the deep things of God is revealed, and you are saturated with the Spirit of truth. This will definitely influence your prayer life as you allow your lips to speak under the anointing of the Holy Spirit.

> *During visitation, the Almighty whispers, "I want to answer your prayers. I will, after I unveil My anointing that flows from My abundance to you."*

Springs of Pleasure

> *All may drink their fill from the delightful springs of Eden* (Psalm 36:8 TPT).

You will find the opportunity arise in His presence to drink deeply of the springs that flow from the Lord. Jesus said, "If anyone thirsts, let him come to Me and drink. He who believes in Me, as the Scripture has said, out of his heart will flow rivers of living water" (John 7:37-38).

Prayer does not have to be an unpleasant experience. The deep fellowship of the presence brings you into springs of everlasting pleasure. The word for "pleasure" used in Psalm 36:8 is the same word used for "Eden," as in the Garden of Eden at creation in the book of Genesis. These flowing streams are within you. According to Jesus, streams within you were present when you became a *believer* in Him. This outflow is eternal life flowing outward from the throne. If you will release yourself to be visited by the Lord in prayer, you may drink of these delightful springs. The life of God will create a wonderful atmosphere to pray and believe for the impossible in your life.

> *Then he showed me the river whose waters give life, sparkling like crystal, flowing out from the throne of God and of the Lamb* (Revelation 22:1 AMPC).

> *During visitation, the Almighty whispers, "I want to answer your prayers. I will, after I unveil My springs of pleasure to you."*

A Fountain of Life

> To know you is to experience a Flowing Fountain, drinking in your life, springing up to satisfy (Psalm 36:9 TPT).

Jesus came to give us life and that life more abundantly (see John 10:10). Do not forget that the heavenly realm is full of life. Life from God will quicken you. The Holy Spirit desires to replenish your life right now. I have had the most amazing times in prayer when this fountain of life became available to me. As I began to have revelation from the Word of God, the Holy Spirit began to reveal the heavenly Father to me. I had the realization the God loves me. Life and healing will begin to flow as we get to know Him. Allow those rivers of living water to flow to you now (see John 7:38).

> *During visitation, the Almighty whispers, "I want to answer your prayers. I will, after I unveil My fountain of life to you."*

Holiness That Brings Revelation

> In the light of your holiness we receive the light of revelation (Psalm 36:9 TPT).

When I was taken to be with the Lord, I was allowed to experience the holiness of the Lord. This holiness of God is the environment of Heaven. This holiness brings such brightness that it releases revelation. The holy fire of God starts to consume anything residing within you that is not of God. It exposes the darkness and drives it away. I received revelation about things in this place that I previously did not see. I have been in this place when I was caught up and stood in His presence. I looked around my feet and there were no shadows. That was how bright it was. Darkness could not abide with this presence. The light exposed everything. Let revelation flow right now to you.

> *During visitation, the Almighty whispers, "I want to answer your prayers. I will, after I unveil My holiness that brings revelation to you."*

Release of Blessings

Lord, keep pouring out your unfailing love on those who are near you. Release more of your blessings to those who are loyal to you (Psalm 36:10 TPT).

God Almighty will release the blessings on you as you yield to His goodness. When He is recognizing your dedication to Him, He will pour out the blessing on you. He wants to bless you as you visit with Him. It is time to receive the blessing of His presence as He stands near you.

Streams of Unfailing Love

One of the most outstanding characteristics of standing before the Lord was His love for me. It flows out from Him like a river. Waves of full acceptance will wash over you as you realize that you were created for a specific purpose. I had full confidence of my value in His eyes. I was part of a very important plan that was too big for me to comprehend. All I had to do was accept His love, and this acceptance was given to begin the amazing process of implementing the divine plan.

> *During visitation, the Almighty whispers, "I want to answer your prayers. I will, after I release My blessings to you and pour out My unfailing love."*

One thing I have desired of the Lord, that will I seek: that I may dwell in the house of the Lord all the days of my life, to behold the beauty of the Lord, and to inquire in His temple. For in the time of trouble He shall hide me in His pavilion; in the secret place of His tabernacle He shall hide me; He shall set me high upon a rock. And now my head shall be lifted up above my enemies all around me; therefore I will offer sacrifices of joy in His tabernacle; I will sing, yes, I will sing praises to the Lord (Psalm 27:4-6).

One Desire

King David sought one thing above everything else—that one thing that he said was "above all else" and was something "I crave" (see Ps. 27:4 TPT). What was it? It was the *secret place*—the special *meeting place with God*. He desired to have God with him all the time. He desired it so much that He wanted to go live with God in His house! He wanted to behold His face and enjoy Him in all of His beauty.

Can you imagine with me what that would be like? You would say, "He is awesome," as He takes your breath away. You can just take Him in all day as you see His glory and encounter His grace.

While in His house, you would immediately realize that you begin to offer up prayers you have already been praying in the secret place. He hears you and is excited to answer your prayers because you are so close to Him.

When you have trouble, you will already have a safe place to hide as you seek refuge in His arms of love. He is so strong and holy. The enemy would not even dare to approach the door.

> *Visitation is not for an audience; it is for participation.*

You Are Safe

You are kept safe and protected in the security of His dwelling. You have made the Most High your dwelling place (see Ps. 91:9). You will be triumphant in everything you do because you stay in the secret place of the Lord. I will make sure that I offer Him praise and adoration as I never hold back from Him. I can experience the overflowing joy of being with Him.

How exciting is it to have a genuine meeting place with God? The Lord has invited you in, and it is time to shout!

> *Yes, listen and you can hear the fanfare of my shouts of praise to the Lord!* (Psalm 27:6 TPT)

You Are Hidden

One of the advantages of being in the secret place is that you are hidden in His presence. This keeps you safe from any evil plan of man that is against you. The secret place will protect you from every evil act or word. You will be so caught up in His presence that you will not hear what man is saying. You will not even know about these plans because you dwell with the Most High!

> *You shall hide them in the **secret place** of Your presence from the plots of man; You shall keep them secretly in a pavilion from the strife of tongues* (Psalm 31:20).

Meeting God face to face in the secret place will deliver you from the fear of man. King Solomon gave us good advice when he said, "The fear of man brings a snare, but whoever trusts in the Lord shall be safe" (Prov. 29:25).

You will need to remember that your reward is with the Lord. You have been privileged to live with Him in this secret place. Therefore, you must realize that you do not need to impress man. Nothing else matters except pleasing Him. Just go and pray in the secret place. Then you will get your answer publicly without saying a word to anyone else.

> *There is a special place in prayer that goes beyond asking or even inquiring. Getting closer to the Lord will require you to enter into the secret place of the Most High. Your goal in your prayer life should not be to "somehow get God to answer your prayer request."*

Even Jesus Himself recommended this when He taught:

> *But you, when you pray, go into your room, and when you have shut your door, pray to your Father who is in the **secret place**; and your Father who sees in **secret** will reward you openly (Matthew 6:6).*

> *When you sit enthroned under the shadow of Shaddai, you are hidden in the strength of God Most High. He's the hope that holds me, and the Stronghold to shelter me, the only God for me, and my great Confidence (Psalm 91:1-2 TPT).*

There is a special place in prayer that goes beyond asking or even inquiring. Getting closer to the Lord will require you to enter into *the secret place of the Most High.* Your goal in your prayer life should not be to "somehow get God to answer your prayer request." If you will really be honest with yourself, most of us think that you must somehow convince or twist God's arm in order to get results in prayer. This is simply not true. At least three things are important factors to consider when we discuss receiving answers through prayer. I want to discuss them in this particular area of *the secret place*. The goal in the *secret place* is not answered prayer; the real goal is fellowship. After engaging God in deep, intimate conversations about the Kingdom of God in deep communion, the Holy Spirit will begin to speak to you specifically about your life, and He will answer your prayers. Sometimes those answers will be provided before you even mention them. Jesus spoke of this in the gospel of Matthew:

> *The goal in the secret place is not just answered prayer; it is fellowship. After engaging God in deep, intimate conversations about the Kingdom of God in deep communion, the Holy Spirit will begin to reveal things to you about your destiny and purpose for life and answer your prayers. Sometimes your answers will come even before you mention the need.*

*So don't worry about these things, saying, "what will we eat? What will we drink? What will we wear?" These things dominate the thoughts of unbelievers, but your heavenly Father **already knows all your needs**. Seek the Kingdom of God above all else, and live righteously, **and he will give you everything you need**. So don't worry about tomorrow, for tomorrow will bring its own worries. Today's trouble is enough for today* (Matthew 6:31-34 NLT).

So after you have had special times of fellowship in the *secret place*, it will be time for the Holy Spirit to begin to engage in prayer by revealing the Father's heart. The Holy Spirit gives words to speak that the Father wants to answer. Because you have chosen to spend time in intimacy, you have captured His heart, and He then is able to take time to address your needs and wants. He is more than willing to give you the Kingdom (see Luke 12:32).

Engage

The Holy Spirit must side with your prayer. He only agrees with what is written in Heaven, which is *every Word* that comes from the mouth of God. Allow Him to speak and counsel you in this intimate setting.

Enforce

Prayer in the Holy Spirit is about domains, dominion, and territories, so you will need to invoke the King's name, King Jesus, when praying. The Holy Spirit may want you to confront strongholds that exist outside your realm of reasoning or senses. You will need to understand your authority as a believer and take a stand against anything that exalts itself against the knowledge of God and bring it into captivity to the knowledge of God (see 2 Cor. 10:5).

Enjoy

You must be dwelling inside the *secret place* and actually praying from the shadow of the cherubim's wings on each side of the Mercy Seat where God is sitting and the blood of Jesus has been placed. You will find that everything is already done for you in Christ, and you will realize that you are free to enjoy the benefits of your salvation instead of trying to be acceptable.

> For the kingdom of God is not eating and drinking, but righteousness and peace and joy in the Holy Spirit. For he who serves Christ in these things is acceptable to God and approved by men (Romans 14:17-18).

One awesome thing to remember about the secret place during *visitation prayer* is that you are protected! You are as close to the Most High as possible, and while you are communing and praying, He will be sure that you are totally protected. In the next chapter, we will break down Psalm 91 verse by verse. Be encouraged that Psalm 91 promises that He will *answer* your prayers and *protect* you while having your *visitation/prayer* time!

Chapter 13

PROTECTION IN PRAYER

When we live our lives within the shadow of the God Most High,
our secret Hiding Place, we will always be shielded from harm!
—PSALM 91:9 TPT

Protected in Visitation Prayer

Our home is with the Most High and our covering is the out-stretched wings of the cherubim. They are positioned on either side of the Mercy Seat where God sits enthroned. The Ark of the Covenant was a replica of a full-sized version in Heaven. God told Moses to be sure to make everything exactly as he had been told on the mountain. Hebrews 8:5 says, "They serve in a system of worship that is only a copy, a shadow of the real one in heaven. For when Moses was getting ready to build the Tabernacle, God gave him this warning: 'Be sure that you make everything according to the pattern I have shown you here on the mountain'" (NLT). I ask you to approach the *throne of grace* and receive mercy now in the shadow of the Most High. "Let us therefore come boldly to the *throne of grace* that we may obtain mercy and find grace to help in time of need" (Heb. 4:16). You are so close that the wings of those mighty angels cast a shadow over you as you feel the comfort of His presence. You begin to pray with a knowing that He will grant you your requests because you just want to spend time with Him.

> *How then could evil prevail against us, or disease infect us?*
> (Psalm 91:10 TPT)

Make sure that you understand how protected you are in this place of *visitation prayer*. You will begin to realize that no evil could ever succeed against you. Anyone who committed evil against you would have to do it in the very presence of the Most High. Prayer and fellowship will happen without any interruption because nothing shall harm you. Not even a disease will be able to infect you. The power and presence of the Holy One will not allow it. Pray on, my beloved. He is your Protector.

> *God sends angels with special orders to protect you wherever*
> *you go, defending you from all harm* (Psalm 91:11 TPT).

Angels are God's fiery messengers that are assigned to serve and care for those who God Himself wills to deliver (see Heb. 1:14 CJB). Angels are only listening to the mighty voice of the Most High. They only want to do His will just as you want to do His will as you stay close to Him in the *secret place*. You are in the secret place. It is then time to make your requests known to Him. The angels are "special forces" on assignment to protect you. They will defend you from all danger. Continue to pursue God in your time of *visitation prayer!*

> *If you walk into a trap, they'll be there for you and keep you*
> *from stumbling!* (Psalm 91:12 TPT)

These "special forces" will be there to walk you through anything the enemy has planned against you. Being in the shadow of the Most High has its benefits. You have these mighty ones that are assigned to guard you.

> *You'll even walk unharmed among the fiercest powers of darkness, trampling every one of them beneath your feet!* (Psalm 91:13 TPT)

Sometimes you will encounter higher-ranking evil spirits that are over regions. Evil spirits that Jesus confronted would beg Him to leave the territory with which they were familiar. Those evil spirits had set up an outpost in the spirit realm to rule over that region. They did not want to give up their position and area of influence. As you walk through these regions, remember that Jesus has said that you will trample over serpents and scorpions and overcome all the power of the enemy (see Luke 10:19).

> *For here is what the Lord has spoken to me: "Because you have delighted in me as my great lover, I will greatly protect you"* (Psalm 91:14 TPT).

The Lord will speak intimate details to you about how your passion toward Him has delighted Him. He will surely protect you from all harm because you have touched His heart. Tell Him how you feel about Him now! He loves you, and now it is time to respond back to Him.

> *It's time to renew your commitment to the Most High God. Let Him know how much you love him and desire Him. Let your soul cry out for help as you consecrate yourself to Him. He really affectionately cares for you. Roll your care over on Him now!*

I will set you in a high place, safe and secure before my face
(Psalm 91:6 TPT).

One of the many benefits of dwelling with the Most High is that if He is in a high place and you are there with Him, then you are also in a high place. It is hard for an enemy to climb up to a high place without being detected and taken out. You are placed in a position of divine protection as you enjoy your security before Him. This verse says that you are "before My face." This clearly means that nothing will go unnoticed and your life will always be safe. It also means that you are going to get what you ask for in prayer. "If you *abide in Me*, and My words *abide in you*, you will ask what you *desire*, and it shall be *done* for you" (John 15:7). "What you desire" is not "what you need." This is where living with God sets you apart. Your prayers will be answered; even the desires of your heart will spring fourth.

My Protection Story

When I was in college, I lived in Broken Arrow, Oklahoma. When I first moved there, I had an apartment near the school. I was accustomed to staying inside and praying for long periods of time. I would interact with my friends when I was not seeking God in these special, designated times. I remember noticing things get so quiet in my neighborhood one night. I knew a storm was coming, but I was not paying attention to it. All of a sudden, I overheard someone with a loudspeaker going from building to building announcing something from the parking lot outside. My phone rang so I answered it. It was my parents calling from Pennsylvania wanting to know how things were doing with my schooling. We talked for a little bit. I think I was so overwhelmed by the heavenly realm that I did not know what was taking place outside.

I heard a freight train coming past my building, and it was so loud. I could feel the vibration as it passed by. I had never noticed train tracks during the day, but I did not investigate now that it was dark. After I hung up with my parents, I continued to seek God. Even though I could tell there was a storm in the area, at the proper time I went to sleep. In the morning, I awoke to pray again. At one point, I pulled open the blinds and glanced out the window. To my surprise, the parking lots were all empty and I was the only one there. I looked straight out, and as far as I could see for miles, there was a trench dug that was at least ten feet deep and forty feet wide. This trench had not been there yesterday. I thought, "God has spared me from a tornado!"

From the path of destruction that it had created, you could see that it had touched down a mile or so away and had come right up to my building. Then, the tornado had lifted up and off the ground and had gone over my building and touched down on the other side and continued onward without hurting me. I even noticed that the building across the street had been hit and the roof was partially missing! It became a notable tornado in the history of that area. I was spared during my time of seeking God when I did not know I was in danger.

Chapter 14

I WILL ANSWER YOU

I will answer your cry for help every time you pray.
—PSALM 91:15 TPT

Because of your intimate relationship with God, you are so close to Him in this "secret place" that He hears your prayers every time you pray. Do not ever worry about a thing. He is working everything out because His desires become your desires. He starts to have great influence upon you as you are transformed in His presence. Even your face is being transformed like Moses's was as you behold His glory. Always be encouraged because your answer is on its way. Remember that you have won His heart because you have made the Most High your dwelling place. *Visitation prayer* is paying off!

> *You will find and feel my presence even in your time of pressure and trouble* (Psalm 91:15 TPT).

When you have your eyes shut, you can still sense someone's presence as they stand near you. That means that they are there even if you cannot see them. In the same way, Jesus will stand with you in your hardest times. He and His angels will be with you to minister to you.

It will increase your faith to know how much He cares for you and wants to get you through all of the pressures and troubles that you face. Let Him visit you in your hard times because His visitation will help to increase your trust in Him. It is time to pray and experience the power of visitation in prayer. "And in that day you will ask Me nothing. Most assuredly, I say to you, whatever you ask the Father in My name *He will give you*. Until now you have asked nothing in My name. Ask, and you will receive, that your joy may be full" (John 16:23-24).

> *I will be your glorious Hero and give you a feast!* (Psalm 91:15 TPT)

Let Jesus be your glorious hero and receive your heart's desires from Him. As you spend time with Him, He will begin to transfer your heart to Him. He wants to honor you before everyone and commend you for trusting in Him. Just have the Lord speak the Word over you, and it will be just as He says. Jesus wants you to yield to the Holy Spirit and fire. You are then purified in His presence. Your faith will rise to a point of telling the Most High, "Speak the word, and it shall be done" (see Luke 7:7). Then He wants to give you a feast in your honor because of your great love for Him.

King David in Psalm 23:5 said, "You prepare a table before me in the presence of my enemies; You anoint my head with oil; my cup runs over." If God is giving a feast for you, do you not think that He wants to give you what you ask of Him? Remember, we are in a relationship with Him. Therefore, you are not in a state of begging in prayer. You have moved into glorious *visitation prayer!*

> **You will be satisfied with a full life and with all that I do for you.**

God wants to bless you with answers and eliminate your questions. The psalmist says that God will satisfy you with a full life. Jesus tells us, "What I am about to do for you is so much more than what you can ask or think that you will be full!"

As the Holy Spirit moves on you now, just repent of doubt and fear. Yield to the faith in the God with whom you have a relationship, and then trust will be rising in your heart. Yield to the mighty Holy Spirit without delay as He comes to you in a great way to help you by revealing Jesus to you. "For you will enjoy the fullness of my salvation!" (Ps. 91:16 TPT).

This is a wonderful statement of God fully answering your prayers. The name *Jesus* is the word for "salvation or deliverance" in Hebrew. So this verse literally says, "For you will enjoy the fullness of my Jesus." I want that! Ever since I met Him in person, I have wanted to experience the "fullness" of Him. There is never a need to worry about anything. He has everything I need and want in His hand. He is visiting with you in the secret place, and He will give you the desires of your heart.

> *Trust in the Lord, and do good; dwell in the land, and feed on His faithfulness. Delight yourself also in the Lord, and* **He shall give you the desires of your heart.** *Commit your way to the Lord, trust also in Him, and He shall bring it to pass. He shall bring forth your righteousness as the light, and your justice as the noonday. Rest in the Lord, and wait patiently for Him* (Psalm 37:3-7).

Do Not Deliver Yourself—He Will!

Jesus wants to have fellowship with you, but you must have victory in all the challenges that come against you as well. Character becomes formed permanently in you because of the places you have experienced as you walk with God. You might think that you have placed yourself within those positions. Regardless of how you arrived in certain situations, He wants you to totally rely on Him. Why do you seek to deliver yourself from those situations? Often, God uses those circumstances to help form our character and create a place of visitation and encounter with God and His purpose. Do not bow to your flesh and your reasoning when you feel pressure or rejection. Have a visitation of the Holy Spirit, and then pray from this place of fellowship with Jesus. Then, after you have been tempted, tested, and tried, you will come out of the cleansing fire as purified silver (see Ps. 12:6) and angels will minister to you (see Matt. 4:11).

> *You are looking for Him to initiate a visitation, but you keep delivering yourself instead of coming to the end of yourself. Trust Him, and know that He will carry you through to completion.*

Chapter 15

REAL WARFARE

It is of utmost importance that you understand this next aspect of prayer. Prayer is also an act of confrontation because of the three previously mentioned demonstrations of the Spirit of God. The Holy Spirit does not hold back concerning who He is and what He represents. Do not take it personally if you find yourself on the wrong side of people or circumstances when the Holy Spirit shows up to help you—He has already picked sides, and you must follow Him with regard to sin, righteousness, and judgment. The Kingdom of God is advancing and confrontation is inevitable. Side with the Holy Spirit, and then you will find victory in your prayer conquests. God wants to answer your prayers—always. Remember that you must confront the world and the evil one with the truth. This is also the work of the Holy Spirit even if it is seldom mentioned by anyone. Jesus said, "But if I cast out demons with the finger of God, surely the kingdom of God has come upon you" (Luke 11:20). It is a sign of the times when we do not hear the full counsel of God from the Word. Paul warned us to be ready for this kind warfare. In the Book of 2 Timothy, he told us what to expect:

For the time will come when they will not endure sound doctrine, but according to their own desires, because they have itching ears, they will heap up for themselves teachers; and they will turn their ears away from **the truth***, and be turned aside to fables. But you be watchful in all things,* **endure afflictions***, do the work of an evangelist, fulfill your ministry* (2 Timothy 4:3-5).

Enemies of Visitation in Prayer

When you feel pressure, do not react as usual. The enemy may have programed you to respond a certain way. It is time to break that conditioned response and react according to who you truly are in Jesus Christ. Identify yourself with the Kingdom of God. Learn to yield to the Holy Spirit and what the Word of the Lord is for the moment. Prayer sometimes becomes a *reactionary* part of our daily life because it becomes *necessary*. God wants it to be *conversational and a continual communion.* You get into the frame of mind that God is always with you! He never leaves you.

> *Let us deal with everything that is an enemy to our visitation during prayer. We need to come to the end of ourselves by bringing into captivity these enemies of our soul.*

Enemies We Must Overcome

Enemy #1: Abandonment

Wage a good fight against *abandonment* with these truths:

1. We are His beloved and have been bought with a price (see 1 Cor. 6:19-20).

2. Jesus prayed for us, that we would be one with the Father as He is one with Him (see John 17:20-23).

3. Jesus called us friends (see John 15:15).

4. Jesus said that we would not be left alone as orphans (see John 14:18).

5. Jesus sent us the Holy Spirit (see John 14:26-27).

6. The Holy Spirit is our Counselor, Helper, Intercessor, Advocate, Strengthener, and Standby.

Enemy #2: Rejection

Wage a good fight against *rejection* with these truths:

1. You are accepted in the Beloved (see Eph. 1:6).

2. You have been bought at a great price (see 1 Cor. 6:20).

3. You are a dearly loved child of God (see Jude 1:1).

4. You have a Father who desires to give you the Kingdom (see Luke 12:32).

Enemy #3: Fear

Wage a good fight against *fear* with these truths:

1. God has given you a spirit of power, love, and a sound mind, not fear (see 2 Tim. 1:7).

2. Perfect love casts out fear because fear involves torment (see 1 John 4:18).

3. "Do not be afraid; I am the First and the Last. I am He who lives, and was dead, and behold, I am alive

forevermore. Amen. And I have the keys of Hades and of Death" (Rev. 1:17-18).

4. Jesus commanded, "Do not be afraid" (Luke 5:10; 8:50; John 6:20).

Enemy #4: Shock and Awe, Deception

These are also known as *lying* signs and wonders by familiar spirits. Wage a good fight against *shock and awe* with these truths:

1. "The coming of the lawless one is according to *the working of Satan, with all power, signs, and **lying wonders**,* and with all unrighteous **deception** among those who perish, because they did not receive the love of the truth, that they might be saved" (2 Thess. 2:9-10).

2. "Do you not know that the unrighteous and the wrongdoers will not inherit or have any share in the kingdom of God? *Do not be deceived (misled)*: neither the impure and immoral, nor idolaters, nor adulterers, nor those who participate in homosexuality, nor cheats (swindlers and thieves), nor greedy graspers, nor drunkards, nor foulmouthed revilers and slanderers, nor extortioners and robbers will inherit or have any share in the kingdom of God" (1 Cor. 6:9-10 AMPC).

3. "Give no regard to mediums and familiar spirits; do not seek after them, to be defiled by them: I am the Lord your God" (Lev. 19:31).

4. "So the great dragon was cast out, that serpent of old, called the Devil and Satan, who deceives the whole world; he was cast to the earth, and his angels were cast out with him" (Rev. 12:9).

5. "For such are false apostles, deceitful workers, transforming themselves into apostles of Christ. And no wonder! For Satan himself transforms himself into an angel of light" (2 Cor. 11:13-14).

6. "Then a spirit came forward and stood before the Lord, and said, 'I will persuade him.' The Lord said to him, 'In what way?' So he said, 'I will go out and be a lying spirit in the mouth of all his prophets.' And the Lord said, 'You shall persuade him, and also prevail. Go out and do so.' Therefore look! The Lord has put a lying spirit in the mouth of all these prophets of yours, and the Lord has declared disaster against you" (1 Kings 22:21-23).

7. "Then the beast was captured, and with him the false prophet who worked signs in his presence, by which he deceived those who received the mark of the beast and those who worshiped his image" (Rev. 19:20).

8. "For your merchants were the great men of the earth, for by your sorcery all the nations were deceived" (Rev. 18:23).

9. "Take heed that you not be deceived. For many will come in My name, saying, 'I am He,' and, 'The time has drawn near.' Therefore do not go after them. But when you hear of wars and commotions, do not be terrified; for these things must come to pass first, but the end will not come immediately" (Luke 21:8-9).

10. "For false messiahs and false prophets will rise up and perform great signs and wonders so as to deceive, if

possible, even God's chosen ones. See, I have warned you about this ahead of time" (Matt. 24:24-25 NLT).

Enemy #5: Trauma (from a Demonic Attack)

Wage a good fight against *trauma* with these truths:

1. "Be sober, be vigilant; because your adversary the devil walks about like a roaring lion, seeking whom he may devour. Resist him, steadfast in the faith, knowing that the same sufferings are experienced by your brotherhood in the world. But may the God of all grace, who called us to His eternal glory by Christ Jesus, after you have suffered a while, perfect, establish, strengthen, and settle you. To Him be the glory and the dominion forever and ever. Amen" (1 Peter 5:8-11).

2. "Then they will deliver you up to tribulation and kill you, and you will be hated by all nations for My name's sake. And then many will be offended, will betray one another, and will hate one another. Then many false prophets will rise up and deceive many. And because lawlessness will abound, the love of many will grow cold. But he who endures to the end shall be saved. And this gospel of the kingdom will be preached in all the world as a witness to all the nations, and then the end will come" (Matt. 24:9-14).

3. "The thief does not come except to steal, and to kill, and to destroy. I have come that they may have life, and that they may have it more abundantly" (John 10:10).

Enemy #6: Doubt

Wage a good fight against *doubt* with these truths:

1. "So Jesus answered and said to them, 'Have faith in God. For assuredly, I say to you, whoever says to this mountain, "Be removed and be cast into the sea," and does not doubt in his heart, but believes that those things he says will be done, he will have whatever he says. Therefore I say to you, whatever things you ask when you pray, believe that you receive them, and you will have them'" (Mark 11:22-24).

2. "Jesus immediately reached out and grabbed him. 'You have so little faith,' Jesus said. 'Why did you doubt me?'" (Matt. 14:31 NLT)

3. "'Why are you frightened?' he asked. 'Why are your hearts filled with doubt?'" (Luke 24:38 NLT)

Enemy #7: Pride

Wage a good fight against *pride* with these truths:

1. "Likewise you younger people, submit yourselves to your elders. Yes, all of you be submissive to one another, and be clothed with humility, for 'God resists the proud, but gives grace to the humble.' Therefore humble yourselves under the mighty hand of God, that He may exalt you in due time, casting all your care upon Him, for He cares for you" (1 Pet. 5:7).

2. "Therefore, as the elect of God, holy and beloved, put on tender mercies, kindness, humility, meekness, longsuffering" (Col. 3:12).

3. "Everyone proud in heart is an abomination to the Lord; though they join forces, none will go unpunished. In mercy and truth atonement is provided for iniquity; and by the fear of the Lord one departs from evil" (Prov. 16:5-6).

Enemy #8: Rebellion (Willful Sin, Iniquity, Hatred, Stubbornness, and Witchcraft)

Wage a good fight against *rebellion* with these truths:

1. "Beware, brethren, lest there be in any of you an evil heart of unbelief in departing from the living God; but exhort one another daily, while it is called 'Today,' lest any of you be hardened through the deceitfulness of sin. For we have become partakers of Christ if we hold the beginning of our confidence steadfast to the end, while it is said: 'Today, if you will hear His voice, do not harden your hearts as in the rebellion'" (Heb. 3:12-15).

2. "For rebellion is as the sin of witchcraft, and stubbornness is as iniquity and idolatry. Because you have rejected the word of the Lord, He also has rejected you from being king" (1 Sam. 15:23).

Enemy #9: Love of the World

Wage a good fight against *love of the world* with these truths:

1. "Do not love the world or the things in the world. If anyone loves the world, the love of the Father is not in him. For all that is in the world—the lust of the flesh, the lust of the eyes, and the pride of life—is not of the Father but is of the world. And the world is passing

away, and the lust of it; but he who does the will of God abides forever" (1 John 2:15-17).

2. "Most assuredly, I say to you, unless a grain of wheat falls into the ground and dies, it remains alone; but if it dies, it produces much grain. He who loves his life will lose it, and he who hates his life in this world will keep it for eternal life. If anyone serves Me, let him follow Me; and where I am, there My servant will be also. If anyone serves Me, him My Father will honor" (John 12:23-26).

3. "Adulterers and adulteresses! Do you not know that friendship with the world is enmity with God? Whoever therefore wants to be a friend of the world makes himself an enemy of God" (James 4:4).

Enemy #10: Unforgiveness

Wage a good fight against *unforgiveness* with these truths:

1. "And when ye stand praying, forgive, if ye have ought against any: that your Father also which is in heaven may forgive you your trespasses. But if ye do not forgive, neither will your Father which is in heaven, forgive your trespasses" (Mark 11:25-26 KJV).

2. "For if ye forgive men their trespasses, your heavenly Father will also forgive you: but if ye forgive not men their trespasses, neither will your Father forgive your trespasses" (Matt. 6:14-15 KJV).

3. "And you, being dead in your trespasses and the uncircumcision of your flesh, He has made alive together

with Him, having forgiven you all trespasses" (Col. 2:13).

> *So ask yourself this question: what do you do to escape the discomfort of coming to the end of yourself?*

"Then Jesus was led up by the Spirit into the wilderness to be tempted by the devil" (Matt. 4:1). Most of us miss the profound truth that is within this verse. When we think of Jesus encountering the devil while on the earth, we think of a desperate entity that is throwing ridiculous options at Jesus. These temptations were valid. The most profound thing of all is that *the Spirit led Jesus into the wilderness to be tempted!*

Jesus yielded to the Holy Spirit and let Him lead. You can be assured that Jesus did not pick and choose which guidance He was going to accept. Jesus did not consider His comfort in situations to be as important as the reason that the Father had in mind while guiding Jesus into them. The supernatural was given opportunity to manifest every time Jesus obeyed in submission to the Father's will, which was revealed by the Spirit. Several truths must be recognized here:

1. Jesus learned obedience from what He suffered, *and so do we* (see Heb. 5:8)!

2. God is creating a showdown with the devil, and He trusts you as being faithful (see Matt. 4:1-2).

3. Your faith and patience are going to be rewarded in temptation. James 1:12 says, "God blesses those who patiently endure testing and temptation. Afterward they will receive the crown of life that God has promised to those who love him" (NLT).

4. You actually will have angels minister to you (see Matt. 4:11).

> *Jesus said to me by the Holy Spirit, "I'm more concerned about your character than your comfort."*

*Beloved, do not think it strange concerning the **fiery trial** which is to try you, as though some strange thing happened to you; but rejoice to the extent that you partake of Christ's sufferings, that when His glory is revealed, you may also be glad with exceeding joy. If you are reproached for the name of Christ, blessed are you, for the **Spirit of glory and of God rests upon you**. On their part He is blasphemed, but on your part He is glorified (1 Peter 4:12-14).*

What does it mean to have the *Spirit of Glory and of God rest upon you*? What does it mean to have a fiery trial? When the pillar of cloud and fire led the Israelites, there were several truths that manifested that will help us in our prayer and visitation time. In the next chapter, let's look in depth at these truths to help understand our life in God and our amazing times of *visitation in prayer*.

Chapter 16

THE WAYS OF VISITATION DURING PRAYER

The ways of God are an immense subject that cannot possibly be written in one book. I would like to focus on a few selected aspects of the Lord's visitations during prayer. Visions, dreams, translation, tongues, and interpretation are all some of the ways of God's visitation. He has impressed me to concentrate on *the angel, the pillar, the cloud, glory, presence, and fire* as catalysts for the next move, not just the gifts of the Spirit.

The next move of God, which has already begun, will be about the revelation of the glory. The glory originates with the Father God and is shared with the Son, who was glorified because of His preexistence involving the redemptive work before the world was created. "And now, O Father, glorify Me together with Yourself, with the glory which I had with You before the world was" (John 17:5). Jesus came and glorified the Father in everything He did. Toward the end of His ministry, Jesus prayed to the Father:

And the glory which You gave Me I have given them, that they may be one just as We are one: I in them, and You in Me; that they may be made perfect in one, and that the world may know that You have sent Me, and have loved them as You have loved Me (John 17:22-23).

The point is that we are to display the glory, which we were given by God the Father. This comes to us as the result of the prayer that Jesus prayed and His redemptive work. We are about to see the manifest sons of God revealed (see Rom. 8:19). The glory of the Father is here in our midst. We have had the Son of God revealed, the Holy Spirit revealed, and now the Father God is being revealed through the glory. He saved the best for last in this last great outpouring.

The Angel of the Lord

The angels have a big part to play in the ways of God. Angels are going to be more prevalent in these last days to reveal the glory of the Father. The Father is going to be more visibly involved with His children in these last days. The angel armies are the military branch of His heavenly government called the Kingdom of God. The Lord briefed me concerning angel activity in these last days. One of those briefings had to do with the increased presence due to His timetable at the end of this dispensation. He said that if His children have not implemented all that was written for a particular time in history, angel activity would increase in order to cause an acceleration to occur. This would cause His body of believers to be positioned correctly for the final outpouring. The angels are masters of transition. If you sense that you are in this transition phase, then be aware that angels are being assigned to help you. Be conscious that they have been sent, and they are everywhere surrounding you.

1. The angel of the Lord is sent on many occasions in the Bible. Angels were sent to protect, give instructions, minister and strengthen, drive out the enemy, and to go before to lead God's people. We need to pay attention and obey the instructions of these heavenly beings.

    *I am sending an **angel** before you **to protect** you on your journey and lead you safely to the place I have prepared for you. **Pay close attention to him, and obey his instructions.** Do not rebel against him, **for he is my representative**, and he will not forgive your rebellion. But if you are **careful to obey him, following all my instructions**, then I will be an enemy to your enemies, and I will oppose those who oppose you. For my angel will go before you and bring you into the land of the Amorites, Hittites, Perizzites, Canaanites, Hivites, and Jebusites, so you may live there. And I will destroy them completely. You must not worship the gods of these nations or serve them in any way or imitate their evil practices. Instead, you must utterly destroy them and smash their sacred pillars. You must serve only the Lord your God. If you do, **I will bless you with food and water**, and **I will protect you from illness**. There will be no miscarriages or infertility in your land, and **I will give you long, full lives. I will send my terror ahead** of you and **create panic among all the people whose lands you invade. I will make all your enemies turn and run. I will send terror ahead of you to drive*** *out* the Hivites, Canaanites, and Hittites (Exodus 23:20-28 NLT).

2. Angels are flames of fire (see Ps. 104:4). They are sent to minister for those who are to inherit salvation (see Heb. 1:14).

Now Moses was tending the flock of Jethro his father-in-law, the priest of Midian. And he led the flock to the back of the desert, and came to Horeb, the mountain of God. And the Angel of the Lord appeared to him in a flame of fire from the midst of a bush (Exodus 3:1-2).

The Pillar

The pillar was a manifestation of God that was a continual reminder that God was with them. The message was loud and clear, "I have got you covered." God was in the pillar (see Exod. 13:21). He is watching over you as well. Just because you do not visibly see it does not mean it is not there. The glory of the Lord will be with you and will help you while you live on this earth. He is teaching you His ways. I can sense His glory cloud right now and it is very strong. You can live in these wonderful ways of visitation. The pillar was both a cloud of His glory by day and a pillar of fire by night. Remember that in your day of visitation—whether you are in the daylight where you can see God moving or you are in your deepest, darkest hour where you can see nothing except the pillar of fire—God will be with you, and He will be guiding you. The Holy Spirit is that pillar, and He can be a cloud or fire in your life. Please meditate on the following truths and let the Holy Spirit speak to you about His ways in your life. I know that Jesus wants you to know that He is with you. He will manifest Himself to you in ways that clearly demonstrate that He is with you.

I can sense, in times of prayer, that He is present with me to lead and guide me in the ways of His Spirit. I know that He wants to show Himself strong on your behalf. There is the mighty covering of God over you. His presence is with you now.

1. **The pillar of cloud and the pillar of fire guided them.** This pillar of cloud and pillar of fire allowed them to travel and be guided by day or night in the wilderness (see Exod. 13:21).

2. **This pillar was always in front of them and was visible** except when the people needed protection from the enemy. That required the pillar to go behind them in order to protect them (see Exod. 13:22).

3. **The angel of God and the pillar of cloud and fire were two different things** (see Exod. 14:19).

4. **God wanted to display His glory by using the pillar and fire against the enemy.** He wanted Pharaoh to chase them. "'And once again I will harden Pharaoh's heart, and he will chase after you. I have planned this in order to display my glory through Pharaoh and his whole army. After this the Egyptians will know that I am the Lord!' So the Israelites camped there as they were told" (Exod. 14:4 NLT).

5. **God was in the fire and pillar cloud.** "But just before dawn the Lord looked down on the Egyptian army from *the pillar of fire and cloud, and he threw their forces into total confusion.* He twisted their chariot wheels,

making their chariots difficult to drive. 'Let's get out of here—away from these Israelites!' the Egyptians shouted. 'The Lord is fighting for them against Egypt!'" (Exod. 14:24-25 NLT)

6. **There was awesome glory displayed before God's people.** "As Aaron spoke to the whole community of Israel, they looked out toward the wilderness. There they could see *the awesome glory of the Lord in the cloud"* (Exod. 16:10 NLT).

The Mountain

The mountain intrigues me as the one thing that can yield to the visitation of the Lord. When you come to the mountain times in your life when you are called to be alone with God, visitation will happen. God will speak as He descends onto the mountain as you wait upon Him. I live on that mountain with God now. I found out that Jesus never intended for us to come down from the mountain with Him, but He intended that we live in that glory as we walk this earth. The Lord requested that all the children of Israel would come up to the mountain and fellowship with Him. The people would not go because of the burning mountain in front of them. Most people I know say they want the fire of God. John the Baptist spoke concerning this fire when referring to Jesus coming after him. He said, "I indeed baptize you with water; but One mightier than I is coming, whose sandal strap I am not worthy to loose. He will baptize you with the Holy Spirit and fire" (Luke 3:16).

Part of the blessing of the outpouring of the Holy Spirit is the baptism of fire. This will increase your purity before the Lord as it concerns your relationship with Him. The blood of Jesus cleanses you from all sin spiritually. Your position with Him is reconciled. However, relationally you are being transformed daily by the renewing of your mind (see

Rom. 12:2). This fire will cause you to walk in this holiness relationally while you live among a vile, perverse generation.

I remember the day when I was asked to go up the mountain of God. I did not immediately understand my calling after becoming born again in 1980. I remember when I was ten years old receiving the call through a vision one night at my Presbyterian church near our house. I used to go to the church at night to pray alone because my family had access to it. I would sit there and tell God that I wanted to do His will as a ten-year-old. One night as I was praying, something left the building that sounded like a scream or a screech, like a bird it flew over me and then left. There was no visible evidence of this, so I continued praying, even though I felt fear.

Then, the vision came. I saw the three seven-year segments of my life flash before my eyes. Each phase was either a training or ministry phase that was ordained by God. I was puzzled because I only saw these three phases. One of them involved seven years of fellowship with God on a mountain of God that was a spiritual situation. I saw myself receiving just as Moses had received up on the mountain. I added up my age of ten to the three phases of seven. This meant that I would be thirty-one years old when I was done with what God had called me to do. Incidentally, at thirty-one years of age, I died and was sent back during a routine surgery. You can read the account in its entirety in the book, *Heavenly Visitation: A Guide to Participating in the Supernatural*.

When I was nineteen, I was asked to go to the highest hill in our area where I lived in Pennsylvania. I frequented that area and was only there for a short while when I was overcome by the presence of God. The Lord told me that I was called to speak for Him. The Lord began to expand on this subject, letting me know those details about what the calling involved. I began to see several powerful gifts of the Holy Spirit manifest in my life. The Lord has used these gifts to help people.

As I left the mountain that evening, I took with me a call of God that requires things that are far beyond my own abilities. It is so sacred that I have never shared it with anyone, and never will. I came down that hill with the gifts and callings of God, which were without repentance. Now when I stand before people, I know that desire that is within them, as well as the intents of their hearts. I know what God is saying to them and how God wants fix their problems. However, most of the time He secretly tells me to teach them the Word and let the seed take root. Sometimes people are not ready to receive all that God desires to give them. When I stand before people who are ready, I go deeper with them and they are given a word because they are seeking God. I have learned that for some it is a lengthy process and for others it is instantaneous. The key here is to obey God when He invites you to the mountain to talk to Him.

Moses testified that the Israelites did not follow God's instructions to come up the mountain. Do not be like those who were afraid to go up the burning mountain and encounter God's ways concerning the holy, cleansing fire when He invited them. "I stood between the Lord and you at that time, to declare to you the word of the Lord; for you were afraid because of the fire, and you did not go up the mountain" (Deut. 5:5). Meditate on the following truths.

1. *The Cloud*

The mountain was a good place for God to visit with Moses. He chose the mountain because of the isolation it afforded to be alone with Moses and to display the fact that He was speaking to Moses from the cloud. He respected Moses. The children of Israel were in disobedience because they too were supposed to come and encounter *visitation on the mountain*. Then the Lord said to Moses:

*I will come to you in a **thick cloud**, Moses, so **the people themselves can hear me when I speak with you**. Then they will always trust you* (Exodus 19:9 NLT).

2. Thunder, Lightning, Dense Cloud, and a Ram's Horn

*On the morning of the third day, **thunder roared and lightning flashed, and a dense cloud came down on the mountain**. There was a long, **loud blast from a ram's horn**, and all the people trembled. Moses led them out from the camp to meet with God, and they stood at the foot of the mountain. All of Mount Sinai was **covered with smoke because the Lord had descended on it in the form of fire**. The smoke billowed into the sky like smoke from a brick kiln, and the **whole mountain shook violently**. As the **blast of the ram's horn** grew louder and louder, **Moses spoke, and God thundered** his reply. **The Lord came down on the top of Mount Sinai** and called Moses to the top of the mountain. So Moses climbed the mountain* (Exodus 19:16-20 NLT).

3. The Dark Cloud

*As the people stood in the distance, Moses approached **the dark cloud where God was*** (Exodus 20:21 NLT).

4. The Glory of the Lord

*Then Moses climbed up the mountain, and the cloud covered it. And **the glory of the Lord settled down on Mount Sinai**, and the cloud covered it for six days. On the seventh day the Lord called to Moses from inside the cloud. To the Israelites at the foot of the mountain, **the glory of the Lord appeared at the summit like a consuming fire**. Then*

*Moses disappeared **into the cloud** as he climbed higher up the mountain. He remained on the mountain forty days and forty nights (Exodus 24:15-18 NLT).*

5. The Lord Was in the Cloud

*Then **the Lord came down in a cloud** and stood there with him; and he called out his own name, Yahweh. The Lord passed in front of Moses, calling out, "Yahweh! The Lord! The God of compassion and mercy! I am slow to anger and filled with unfailing love and faithfulness. I lavish unfailing love to a thousand generations. I forgive iniquity, rebellion, and sin. But I do not excuse the guilty. I lay the sins of the parents upon their children and grandchildren; the entire family is affected—even children in the third and fourth generations."*

*Moses immediately threw himself to the ground and worshiped. And he said, "O Lord, if it is true that I have found favor with you, then please travel with us. Yes, this is a stubborn and rebellious people, but please forgive our iniquity and our sins. **Claim us as your own special possession**." The Lord replied, "**Listen, I am making a covenant with you in the presence of all your people. I will perform miracles that have never been performed anywhere in all the earth or in any nation. And all the people around you will see the power of the Lord—the awesome power I will display for you**. But listen carefully to everything I command you today" (Exodus 34:5-11 NLT).*

Tent of Meeting

1. *The Lord would speak face to face with Moses.*

*Whenever Moses went out to the Tent of Meeting, all the people would get up and stand in the entrances of their own tents. They would all watch Moses until he disappeared inside. As he went into the tent, **the pillar of cloud would come down and hover at its entrance** while the Lord spoke with Moses. When the people saw the cloud standing at the entrance of the tent, they would stand and bow down in front of their own tents. Inside the Tent of Meeting, **the Lord would speak to Moses face to face, as one speaks to a friend.** Afterward Moses would return to the camp, but the young man who assisted him, Joshua son of Nun, would remain behind in the Tent of Meeting (Exodus 33:8-11 NLT).*

2. *The cloud covered and the glory filled.*

*Then **the cloud covered the Tabernacle, and the glory of the Lord filled the Tabernacle.** Moses could no longer enter the Tabernacle because the cloud had settled down over it, and the glory of the Lord filled the Tabernacle. Now whenever the cloud lifted from the Tabernacle, the people of Israel would set out on their journey, following it. But if the cloud did not rise, they remained where they were until it lifted. **The cloud of the Lord hovered over the Tabernacle** during the day, and **at night fire glowed inside the cloud** so the whole family of Israel could see it. This continued throughout all their journeys (Exodus 40:34-38 NLT).*

I just wanted to share with you the desire of the Trinity for your life. I have met Jesus and want to convey the intimacy that is waiting for you. When He stood before me, I realized that nothing else mattered in this life except to please Him. Your reward is based on your heartfelt love for Him that caused you to manifest God's purpose in your life. Faith rises when revelation rises. The greatest revelation that you can have on this earth is the love of God. He loves you and wants you all to Himself. When Moses would leave the Tent of Meeting, Joshua would stay and lie in God's presence continually.

> Inside the Tent of Meeting, **the Lord would speak to Moses face to face, as one speaks to a friend.** Afterward Moses would return to the camp, but the young man who assisted him, Joshua son of Nun, would remain behind in the Tent of Meeting (Exodus 33:11 NLT).

Most Holy Place

1. *The Lord Himself is present in the cloud above the Ark.*

> The Lord said to Moses, "Warn your brother, Aaron, not to enter the Most Holy Place behind the inner curtain whenever he chooses; if he does, he will die. For the Ark's cover—the place of atonement—is there, and **I myself am present in the cloud above the atonement cover**" (Leviticus 16:2 NLT).

The Most Holy place contained the Ark of the Covenant. As you enter into this area of prayer, remember that He is present over the atonement cover. Place yourself before Him and know that your sins are atoned forever when you continually come before Him in humility and adoration.

2. Clouds of incense will rise over the Ark.

*Aaron will present his own bull as a sin offering to purify himself and his family, making them right with the Lord. After he has slaughtered the bull as a sin offering, he will fill an incense burner with burning coals from the altar that stands before the Lord. Then he will take two handfuls of fragrant powdered incense and will carry the burner and the incense behind the inner curtain. **There in the Lord's presence he will put the incense on the burning coals so that a cloud of incense will rise over the Ark's cover— the place of atonement—that rests on the Ark of the Covenant.** If he follows these instructions, he will not die. Then he must take some of the blood of the bull, dip his finger in it, and sprinkle it on the east side of the atonement cover. He must sprinkle blood seven times with his finger in front of the atonement cover* (Leviticus 16:11-14 NLT).

As you begin to worship Him, you are sprinkling incense on the burning coals from the sacrificial alter. Your prayers and worship create a cloud that rises to God. You are in a perfect position now as the prayers and worship ascend to Him.

3. There is a regular pattern of cloud and fire.

*On the day the Tabernacle was set up, **the cloud covered it**. But from evening until morning **the cloud** over the Tabernacle looked like **a pillar of fire**. This was the regular pattern—at night the cloud that covered the Tabernacle had the **appearance of fire*** (Numbers 9:15-16 NLT).

It is important to note that the fire and the cloud were over the Tabernacle consistently. God is protecting you as well as visiting with you.

4. ***The temple is a place for God to dwell.***

> *When the priests came out of the Holy Place, **a thick cloud filled the Temple of the Lord**. The priests could not continue their service because of the cloud, for the glorious presence of the Lord filled the Temple of the Lord. Then Solomon prayed, "O Lord, you have said that you would **live in a thick cloud of darkness**. Now I have built **a glorious Temple** for you, a place where you can live forever!"*
> (1 Kings 8:10-13 NLT)

Eventually God will come into your life in such a way that you are overwhelmed with His presence. He has filled places so strongly that I have had to crawl because I could not walk. I have had to sit down because when He comes in you cannot stand any longer. I remember this happening so many times at church. I have had the pastor crawl on his hands and knees to get to me because he had a word for me. The presence was so strong that it was easier to crawl than walk. My wife and I are constantly overcome in our home with His visitation. This is what He desires for all His people.

Jesus

1. ***There was a bright cloud of glory.***

> *But even as he spoke, **a bright cloud** overshadowed them, and a voice from the cloud said, "This is my dearly loved Son, who brings me great joy. Listen to him." The disciples were terrified and fell face down on the ground. Then Jesus came over and touched them. "Get up," he said. "Don't be afraid." And when they looked up...**they saw only Jesus*** (Matthew 17:5-8 NLT).

2. Jesus was taken up on the cloud.

*After saying this, he was **taken up into a cloud** while they were watching, and they could no longer see him. As they strained to see him rising into heaven, two white-robed men suddenly stood among them. "Men of Galilee," they said, "why are you standing here staring into heaven? Jesus has been taken from you into heaven, but someday he will return from heaven in the same way you saw him go!" (Acts 1:9-11 NLT)*

3. Jesus will return on the cloud.

*Then everyone will see **the Son of Man coming on a cloud with power and great glory.** So when all these things begin to happen, stand and look up, for your salvation is near! (Luke 21:27-28 NLT)*

4. Jesus was seated on the cloud.

*Then I saw a **white cloud,** and seated on the cloud was someone like **the Son of Man.** He had a gold crown on his head and a sharp sickle in his hand (Revelation 14:14 NLT).*

Jesus is surrounded by the glory of the Father. He prayed in John 17 that we would have that same glory. I remember seeing this glory around me. Jesus promises us that we have the glory that was given to Him.

I recall several years ago when Jesus appeared to me in Phoenix, Arizona. We were completely immersed in the process of moving to New Orleans full time. Our house had sold so quickly that we had to stay with friends for a couple of months. Jesus came to me in the early morning hour and stood by my bed. I saw that He had a beautiful horn that looked like my soprano saxophone. I had learned how to play instruments supernaturally, and the saxophone was one of them. He began to play the most anointed melodies on that sax as I lay there on my bed. I was overcome by the presence as He played. Suddenly, He stopped and handed me the sax. He said, "You play it now for Me."

I told Him that when I play the sax, it does not even compare with what He had just played. He explained to me that I could play that way if I desired. As He began to teach me how to play, I noticed a blue and gold cloud all around me. He said, "The breath of Heaven is always available to you. You can see it around you like a cloud. Before you play your instrument, breathe in this breath of Heaven." So I breathed it in and exhaled it through the horn. To my surprise, the horn played the sounds of Heaven just as well as Jesus had played them.

Be encouraged as you walk in this life. The breath of Heaven is all around you. All you need to do is inhale Heaven's glory and exhale the glory as you walk through whatever the Lord has called you to do in victory.

Chapter 17

TURNING EVERYTHING OVER TO HIM

This is what you should ask this during visitation and prayer:
"Lord, what do You want me to do in this situation?"

How many times have we all told the Lord our heartfelt commitment to Him only to go suddenly into what I call "survival mode"? When the enemy comes in to stop our momentum, we sometimes automatically click over, curl into a little ball, and cower. There are specialized "momentum breakers." They are caused by evil spirits that are sent to break our pace-setting stride in our *faith race*. We need to program ourselves to respond correctly. The Author and Finisher of our faith is *waiting to execute a supernatural event in your life!*

When we have the proper response, which is the secret code of God's Word coming from our lips, even though we are under pressure all of the angels have already been told the code words. When you speak these words, they match what Jesus has already spoken, and the *special forces* of the angel armies are set in motion on your behalf. They harken unto the voice of the Lord and do His bidding. You cannot lose as you begin to flow in the supernatural realms of God!

Our response during a time of turning everything over to God is called a *prayer of dedication and consecration. Visitation prayer* includes those times when you yield all of the concern to God and ask Him for understanding. God has a planned response to every situation. He wants to engage you on a more intimate level and answer your prayers from a supernatural point of view. He wants to help you in this way.

> *When we were praying to find our house, this prophecy came forth twice, "I'm not hiding your house from you. I'm hiding the house for you!" He got it for us. It was being hidden just for us!*

I remember when we were looking for a house in New Orleans after the Lord had called us to live there. We would come down and stay in a hotel every month for two weeks at a time. We did that for several months and could not find the right house. We prayed in the Holy Spirit for hours each day, and then we would return to Phoenix to work for the remainder of each month. Finally, the answer arrived. The answer came only after continually offering thanksgiving to God, sowing financially into our church, and praying forth the mysteries in the Spirit. On separate occasions, we had two friends tell us that the Lord had the house and that He was hiding it for us, not hiding it from us. Then suddenly, our answer came to us supernaturally. We could not do it on our own, and He came through for us.

> *We find ourselves being overcome by our cares, but not overcome by His presence. This should not be!*

You may ask, "What does God have for me that is the very answer I am seeking?" He is waiting for the right timing to reveal it to you. He is waiting for the right timing when you respond in faith! God wants you to have the answers to your prayers *when you cast the care of it on Him.* He cares for you so deeply (see 1 Pet. 5:7). Often, we find ourselves being overcome by our cares but not overcome by His presence. This should not be. What is it you need from Him? He is not withholding it from you. He is waiting for you to worship and thank Him for what He already wants to do for you. Let God have any space inside your soul that is not His. Give Him the space! Turn it over to Him and experience His visitation in your prayers.

> *God has something you need. What is it within you that He wants that you have not turned over to Him?*

Sometimes our prayers are not answered because we are looking at what we need and not at what God wants. He loves His people and wants to give them the Kingdom. But He also knows that He cannot dwell with you intimately if there are things that are in the way. He is the *high and lofty One* and rules in eternity on high. He also dwells with the meek and humble person who yields to Him continually. The Spirit of God through the prophet Isaiah says that we have to humble ourselves and have repentant hearts.

> *The high and lofty one who lives in eternity, the Holy One, says this: "I live in the high and holy place with those whose spirits are contrite and humble. I restore the crushed spirit of the humble and revive the courage of those with repentant hearts. For I will not fight against you forever; I will not always be angry. If I were, all people would pass away— all the souls I have made"* (Isaiah 57:15-16 NLT).

We will receive in prayer *everything we ask* when God dwells with us. The act of handing over everything during visitation and allowing Him to move in and live with you will produce the greatest efficiency in prayer. The Holy Spirit will honor the covenant you have with the Most High and will not let you ask amiss. God will certainly respond to your requests as you visit with Him. He loves you, and you love Him. This makes your joy full (see John 15:11). Because you abide in Him and He abides in you, He gives you *whatever you desire*.

> *If you abide in Me, and My words abide in you, you will ask what **you desire**, and it shall be done for you. By this My Father is glorified, that you bear much fruit; so you will be My disciples* (John 15:7-8).

> **You have got to yield and humble yourself. God resists the proud. When you resist the devil you do not comply with the enemy's demands—you resist him completely. In the same way, God resists—He pushes back the proud, but He gives grace to the humble.**

The idea of yielding has to do with *authority*. Yielding to someone greater than you in authority is called *submission*. The overpowering presence that you encounter in visitation prayer has an effect on your authority because the Greater One begins to influence you as you yield to Him. Unyielding people resist the Lord's will instead of yielding completely to Him. God resists the proud as well. He resists them (see James 4:6). We are to resist the devil, not God (see James 4:7). I yield and humble myself now because I want to receive grace. How about you? Do you want to receive grace? If so, humble yourself and yield to God.

> **God is positioning you in a place where you can receive everything that He has for you.**

During *visitation*, prayer comes so easily because the Lord is the One who is visiting you. It does not come easily just because of who you are to Him. As you spend time with Him, He becomes your dwelling place. Prayer is no longer begging God for help; *prayer becomes communion with Him.* It is a place where you reveal the secrets of your heart and the covenant becomes active. Because God is greater, you benefit from the covenant because He brings more into the relationship than you do. That is good; so do not worry about your needs or wants. He has you covered. That is the purpose of the covenant. *All we need is to develop a relationship with Him through visitation, and that will cause faith to be cultivated.* "And it is impossible to please God without faith. Anyone who wants to come to him must believe that God exists and that he rewards those who sincerely seek him" (Heb. 11:6 NLT). *The shift comes when faith springs forth and you know that nothing is impossible to those who believe* (see Mark 9:23).

> **The Spirit is the One who knows what you really need.**

Things never discovered or heard of before, things beyond our ability to imagine—these are the many things God has in store for all his lovers. But God now unveils these profound realities to us by the Spirit. Yes, he has revealed to us his inmost heart and deepest mysteries through the Holy Spirit, who constantly explores all things. After all, who can really see into a person's heart and know his hidden impulses except for that person's spirit. **So it is with God. His thoughts and secrets are only fully understood by** *his Spirit, the Spirit of God. For we did not receive the spirit of this world system but the Spirit of God, so that we might come to understand and experience all that grace has lavished upon us. And we articulate these realities with the words imparted to us by the Spirit and not with the words taught by human wisdom. We join together Spirit-revealed truths with Spirit-revealed words. Someone living on an entirely human level rejects the revelations of God's Spirit, for they make no sense to him. He can't understand the revelations of the Spirit because they are only discovered by the illumination of the Spirit. Those who live in the Spirit are able to carefully evaluate all things, and they are subject to the scrutiny of no one but God. For Who has ever intimately known the mind of the Lord Yahweh well enough to become his counselor? Christ has, and we possess Christ's perceptions* (1 Corinthians 2:10-16 TPT).

It is amazing to me how resistant the *natural man* is to the unseen spiritual realm. It is especially obvious the resistance has to do with things that concern faith and the Kingdom. However, it appears that we will readily believe the "god of this world," or realm, when he lies to us just because we can encounter these things and see them with our eyes. What we see down here in the earthly realm may appear to be a fact, but it is certainly not always the truth!

> *Turn to Him in the darkest hour—God is preparing you completely so that the supernatural can occur in your life.*

Have you ever noticed how hard it is to pray in the *dark hours* of your life? You are usually grieved by situations you are facing and do not always feel like turning to God because of these feelings. However, when you are hurting and in trouble, that is the very time that you need to turn to Him. "Therefore humble yourselves under the mighty hand of God, that He may exalt you in due time, casting all your care upon Him, for He cares for you" (1 Peter 5:6-7). The most important thing to remember about the heavenly realm is that you must yield to that realm. When you do yield to the heavenly realm, the Comforter will visit you. Prayer will become a breath of Heaven as you effectively pray by the Spirit. "But the Comforter *(Counselor, Helper, Intercessor, Advocate, Strengthener, Standby)*, the Holy Spirit, Whom the Father will send in My name [in My place, to represent Me and act on My behalf], He will teach you all things" (John 14:26 AMPC).

The word *Comforter* (Strong's number G3875) is the Greek word *parakletos* (par-ak'-lay-tos), which means an intercessor, consoler. Here are the six words that the Amplified Bible uses to describe the word *Comforter*.

Counselor

Webster's Dictionary describes a counselor as being, "any person who gives advice; but properly one who is authorized by natural relationship, or by birth, office or profession, to advise another in regard to his future conduct and measures." It could also mean "one appointed to advise a king or chief magistrate, in regard to the administration of the government or one who is consulted by a client in a law case; one who gives advice in relation to a question of law; one whose profession is to give advice in law, and manage causes for clients."

Helper

Webster's Dictionary describes a helper as being, "One that helps, aids or assists; and assistant; an auxiliary. One that furnishes or administers a remedy. When the supplies with anything wanted; a helper to a husband; a supernumerary servant."

Intercessor

Webster's Dictionary describes an *intercessor* as being:

1. A mediator; one who interposes between parties at variance, with a view to reconcile them; one who pleads in behalf of another.

2. A bishop who, during a vacancy of the see, administers the bishopric till a successor is elected.

Advocate

Webster's Dictionary describes an *advocate* (from the Latin meaning to call for, to plead for, to call):

1. *Advocate,* in its primary sense, signifies one who pleads the cause of another in a court of civil law.

2. One who pleads the cause of another before any tribunal or judicial court, as a barrister in the English courts. In English and American courts, advocates are the same as counsel, or counselors.

3. One who defends, vindicates, or espouses a cause, by argument; one who is friendly to; as, and advocate for peace, or for the oppressed.

4. In Scripture, Christ is called an advocate for his people. We have an advocate with the Father (see 1 John 2:1).

5. Verb transitive: to plead in favor of; to defend by argument, before a tribunal; to support or vindicate.

Strengthener

Webster's Dictionary describes a *strengthener* as being:

1. That which increases strength, physical or moral.

2. In medicine, something which taken into the system, increases the action and energy of the vital powers.

Standby

A *standby* is one who is instantly ready to act for the benefit of the one assigned to or to assist.

Answered Prayer

It's interesting to note the way the Jesus speaks about prayer. He says:

> *Most assuredly, I say to you, he who believes in Me, the works that I do he will do also; and greater works than these he will do, because I go to My Father. And whatever you ask in My name, that I will do, that the Father may be glorified in the Son. If you ask anything in My name, I will do it* (John 14:12-14).

I want to emphasize that the first thing He powerfully says is *most assuredly I say to you.* This is said with the upmost confidence that you can possibly infer. What Jesus is saying is going to happen, and it is the absolute truth (a "timeless truth" in *The Passion Translation*).

So, the number-one truth that we need to remember is this one: "He who believes in Me, the works that I do he will do also." According to how Jesus started this conversation, it has already been fully accomplished. He also said that even "greater works" than the ones that He did they will do because He went to the Father. Jesus goes on to state, with the same assurance and confidence, that when you *ask anything*—whatever it is ("whatever" means without any limitations)—Jesus *will* do it for you so that the Father would be glorified. He then states again, just to emphasize the fact, that if we ask anything in His name He will do it for us. Honestly, these verses only have one prerequisite—to *believe in Him.*

I have to tell you that meeting Him face to face has changed me. The things that He said now define me. When He's talking to you and you are looking into His eyes, everything He says works to define you. His words actually go in and burn or imprint an image of Himself in you. This image is imprinted so completely that the impossible becomes possible. If the Creator and Ruler of the universe tells you, "If you believe in Me, you will do the works that I do and even greater works," and that if you "ask anything in My name" it will be done, then it is not just a matter of hearing Him saying it. It is the very truth that He has burned within you, and it becomes part of you. Then it is no longer just truth; it is a living Word inside of you. I used to have a hard time with faith, which means believing God, until I realized that Jesus Himself confirms everything that was set in Heaven and is written on the earth. His words are not just something you hear; they are something that you eat. They become part of you and grow. Truth can become a reality. This reality is based on a relationship, not on just your position with Him. I may have a position and work for someone, but it is not the same as having a relationship with someone on a personal level. If you work for someone, you may just do what he or she tells you to do and go home every night. You do not become as they are, necessarily, unless you are being mentored in that relationship.

After spending time with Jesus, you find yourself doing the same things that Jesus did when He was on the earth—and even greater things! You find yourself, in prayer, asking because of your relationship and not just your position. This is why I have emphasized having *visitation* first and then *praying*. Having that fellowship and communion with Him is of far greater importance than most people realize. Prayer results after there is communion and fellowship because the relationship then brings visitation to a new level. It brings the relationship to a point where you easily share intimate secrets with each other. God wants to do anything you ask because of the relationship you have with Him, not just because of your position with Him. Here is the full passage in John from *The Passion Translation*:

> *"I tell you this timeless truth: The person who follows me in faith, believing in me, will do the same mighty miracles that I do—even greater miracles than these because I go to be with my Father! For I will do whatever you ask me to do when you ask me in my name. And that is how the Son will show what the Father is really like and bring glory to him. Ask me anything in my name, and I will do it for you!"*

> *"Loving me empowers you to obey my commands. And I will ask the Father and he will give you another **Savior, the Holy Spirit of Truth**, who will be to you **a friend** just like me—and he will never leave you. The world won't receive him because they can't see him or know him. But you will know him intimately, because he will make his home in you and will live inside you."*

> *"I promise that I will never leave you helpless or abandon you as orphans—I will come back to you! Soon I will leave this world and they will see me no longer, but you will see me, because I will live again, and **you will come alive too**. So when that day comes, you will know that I am living in the Father and that you are one with me, for I will be living in you. Those who truly love me are those who obey my commandments. Whoever passionately loves me will be passionately loved by my Father. And I will passionately love you in return and will manifest my life within you."*

Then one of the disciples named Judas (not Judas the locksmith) said, "Lord, why is it you will only reveal Your identity to us and not to everyone?"

Jesus replied, "Loving me empowers you to obey my word. And my Father will love you so deeply that we will come to you and make you our dwelling place. But those who don't love me will not obey my words. The Father did not send me to speak my own revelation, but the words of my Father. I am telling you this while I am still with you. But when the Father sends the Spirit of Holiness, the One like me who sets you free, he will teach you all things in my name. And he will inspire you to remember every word that I've told you" (John 14:12-26 TPT).

> **The Holy Spirit is my help. He is my Counselor.**

Jesus Promises the Defense Attorney

When you love someone deeply, you will do anything for him or her that you can. Loving someone allows you to go further in a relationship. Your will is influenced by what you believe about someone. Jesus wants your love for Him to propel you into submission and obedience to His commandments. He said to take His yoke upon yourself and let Him help you because His burden is light (see Matt. 11:28-29). If you genuinely love someone, your actions will prove that love exists.

Jesus has announced that Someone is coming who is like Him. The Spirit is the true Holy One who stands by to help and to defend us. He will tell you the truth and defend you in this world so that you do not need to ever be alone. When He is allowed to live through us, He can cause us to triumph in every situation. The apostle Paul said,

"Now thanks be to God who always leads us in triumph in Christ, and through us diffuses the fragrance of His knowledge in every place" (2 Cor. 2:14). Having this Defender will cause you to win every case; it will cause your prayer life to go to its optimum level.

> ### *Enter into My glory. Walk with Me like never before.*

Jesus reiterates in John 14:21, "Those who truly love me are those who obey my commandments. Whoever passionately loves me will be passionately loved by my Father. And I will passionately love you in return and will *manifest my life within you*" (TPT). Do you see why visitation is so important in getting your prayers answered? I will do anything that He commands to prove my love for Him. In return, He will passionately return that love and manifest Himself within me. He "sends the Spirit of Holiness, the One like me who sets you free" (John 14:26 TPT).

Jesus has set you free from the curse. Now, the Holy One was sent to strengthen that freedom that resides within us and deliver us continually. It is time to reconcile and receive the gift of answered prayer!

> ### *What has been paid for already? Reconcile,*
> ### *and take that which He has given to you.*

Chapter 18

WALKING IN THE POWER OF VISITATION AND PRAYER

By his divine power, God has given us everything we need for living a godly life. *We have received all of this by coming to know him, the one who called us to himself by means of his marvelous glory and excellence. And because of his glory and excellence, he has given us great and precious promises. These are the promises that enable you to share his divine nature and escape the world's corruption caused by human desires.*

In view of all this, make every effort to respond to God's promises. Supplement your faith with a generous provision of moral excellence, and moral excellence with knowledge, and knowledge with self-control, and self-control with patient endurance, and patient endurance with godliness, and godliness with brotherly affection, and brotherly affection with love for everyone.

The more you grow like this, the more productive and useful you will be in your knowledge of our Lord Jesus Christ. But those who fail to develop in this way are shortsighted or blind, forgetting that they have been cleansed from their old sins.

So, dear brothers and sisters, work hard to prove that you really are among those God has called and chosen. Do these things, and you will never fall away. Then God will give you a grand entrance into the eternal Kingdom of our Lord and Savior Jesus Christ (2 Peter 1:3-11 NLT).

The power of God's visitation translates into our prayer life and every other part of our life as well. This fellowship and communion transforms us as we begin to manifest characteristics of our heavenly Father into this realm. People begin to see the difference in our lives that is a result of spending time with the Lord. Moses spent so much time with God in communion and fellowship that he began to have beams of glory coming out of his face as he went about his daily activities around others. People actually asked him to put a veil on his face because they were afraid (see Exod. 34:29-33). The apostle James said, "Show me your faith without your works, and I will show you my faith by my works" (James 2:18). Any true transaction between the natural realm and the realm of Heaven will have a manifestation from one realm to the other. The supernatural realm is real and much more powerful than this natural realm. We must yield to the supernatural by exercising our humility and faith to cause things to begin to be transferred from the heavenly realm to our natural realm.

When I met Jesus face to face, I realized that He was exceedingly powerful as a person. His personality is characteristic of the power of the Holy Spirit. So the same Spirit who was in Jesus is same Spirit who was given on the day of Pentecost. The words that Jesus speaks are very powerful. They create substance within you. They can create character because they start as a seed, and then they grow within you. I realized that the reason I was not receiving manifestations as a result of my prayer time was because I did not accept the Word of God humbly as the incorruptible Word. Peter said, "Being born again, not of corruptible seed, but of incorruptible, by the word of God, which liveth and abideth for ever" (1 Pet. 1:23 KJV). When I started to have times of visitation during prayer, allowing the Holy Spirit to minister to me concerning the Word of God, answers came because I was humble and accepted the seed of the Word into my heart. The words sprouted up, and then I began to see a harvest in my life, all because of visitation, humility, and the seed of the Word being planted and manifesting. The Lord requires us to live humbly before Him and accept the Word planted in us. James 1:21 says, "So get rid of all the filth and evil in your lives, and humbly accept the word God has planted in your hearts, for it has the power to save your souls" (NLT).

> *He has shown you, O man, what is good; and what does the Lord require of you but to do justly, to love mercy, and to walk humbly with your God?* (Micah 6:8)

Eight Godly Attributes to Walk In

Faith

Webster's Dictionary describes *faith* as:

1. An affectionate practical confidence in the testimony of God.

2. A firm, cordial belief in the veracity of God, in all the declarations of his word; for a full and affectionate

confidence in the certainty of those things which God
has declared, and because he has declared them.

One of the powerful attributes of your walk with God during visitation is your faith. Without faith, it is impossible to please God (see Heb. 11:6). This attribute is very important in your walk with Father God. Faith pertains to the unseen world. My faith is a conviction of the unseen realm of God and what God says about His realm. God also reveals Himself through His Word, and that revelation brings forth a trust in Him. You will see a strong conviction arise in your heart as you mature into this attribute called faith.

Moral Excellence

Webster's Dictionary describes *moral* as:

> Relating to the practice, manners or conduct of men as
> social beings in relation to each other, and with reference to right and wrong. The word moral is applicable to
> actions that are good or evil, virtuous or vicious, when
> has reference to the law of God as the standard by which
> their character is to be determined. The word however
> may be applied to actions, which affect only, or primarily
> and principally, a person's own happiness.

When you walk in the power of God, you will begin to manifest the character of God in all that you do. Behavior will start to be influenced by the power of God concerning what God is doing in you that affects your interaction with others and not just you personally. Jesus will want you to treat others as you would want to be treated. Your standards of moral excellence will absolutely be influenced by the power of God, which will cause you to represent the Kingdom of God in your walk with Him. The world will recognize that you are walking in a higher realm because of your moral excellence.

Knowledge

Webster's Dictionary describes *knowledge* as:

1. A clear and certain perception of that which exists, or of truth and the fact; the perception of the connection and agreement, or disagreement and repugnancy of our ideas. We can have no knowledge of that which does not exist. God has a perfect knowledge of all his works. Human knowledge is very limited, and is mostly gained by observation and experience.

2. Learning; illumination of mind.

To know God is to know His ways. Many people observe Him and His acts, but true knowledge is when we perceive the truth and character of God. "He made *known His ways* to Moses, His acts to the children of Israel" (Ps. 103:7 NKJV). God has given us His Holy Spirit to give us this knowledge by revelation (see Eph. 1:17-18). The power of the Spirit of God will manifest as you walk with Him in *visitation*.

Self-Control (Restraint)

Webster's Dictionary describes *restraint* (self-control) as:

The active operation of holding back or hindering from motion, in any manner; hindrance of the will, or of any action, physical, moral or mental.

Many of us have experienced a situation where it was not the correct time to take action or even speak a word. It takes great discipline to walk in self-control in this life. When the Spirit of God comes in power in your life, you have no choice but to yield to Him. He is a beautiful person who is your answer to the flesh and lack of restraint. As you yield your will to Him, the Holy Spirit gives you a tremendous visitation. This will happen as you choose Him over your present circumstance.

Patient Endurance

Webster's *Dictionary* describes *endurance* as:

> Continuance; a state of lasting or duration; lastingness. A bearing or suffering; a continuing under pain or distress without resistance, or without sinking or yielding to the pressure; sufferance; patience.

We all encounter stress and pressure in this life on earth. Add to that the pain that may accompany these situations and it will cause suffering. When we endure these circumstances patiently, the wind of the Spirit will come and build us up and cause us to stand. The Lord will reward you for your faithfulness. He will visit you! "Therefore do not cast away your confidence, which has great reward. For you have need of *endurance*, so that after you have done the will of God, you may receive the promise" (Heb. 10:35-36).

Godliness

Webster's *Dictionary* describes *godliness* as:

> 1. Piety; belief in God, and reverence for his character and laws.
>
> 2. A religious life; a careful observance of the laws of God and performance of religious duties, proceeding from love and reverence for the divine character and commands; Christian obedience. Godliness is profitable unto all things.

One of the most amazing attributes of our powerful walk in the spirit is being God-like. We are like our Father God as His children. As we walk with God, we start to act like Him because of the effects of association. We also have His spiritual DNA in us because of the New Birth. This all works in our favor as the mighty Holy Spirit comes in power and transforms us as we walk with Him. "Therefore be *imitators of God* as dear children. And walk in love, as Christ also has loved us and given Himself for us, an offering and a sacrifice to God for a sweet-smelling aroma" (Eph. 5:1-2).

Brotherly Affection (Affectionate)

Webster's *Dictionary* describes *affectionate* as:

1. Having great love or affection; fond; as an affectionate brother.

2. Warm in affection; zealous. Man, in his love to God, and desire to please him; can never be too affectionate.

3. Proceeding from affection; indicating love; benevolent; tender; as, the affectionate care of a parent; an affectionate countenance.

4. Inclined to; warmly attached.

One of the signs that Jesus gave concerning the end-time scenario was the lack of affection and concern for others. With this powerful walk in the spirit of visitation, you will find yourself affectionately caring for others without any effort. This will be a sign to the unbelieving generation that God is walking with us. Jesus said, "Sin will be rampant everywhere, and the *love of many will grow cold*. But the one who endures to the end will be saved" (Matt. 24:11-13 NLT).

Love

Webster's *Dictionary* describes *love* as:

1. An affection of the mind excited by beauty and worth of any kind, or by the qualities of an object which communicate pleasure, sensual or intellectual. It is opposed to hatred.

2. The love of God is the first duty of man, and this springs from just views of his attributes or excellencies of character, which afford the highest delight in the sanctified heart. Esteem and reverence constitute ingredients in this affection, and a fear of offending him is its inseparable affect.

Love was expressed by the Godhead through the salvation of man. We are to love God with this powerful truth in the forefront of our thinking and in everything we do and say. You are to "love the Lord your God with all your heart, with all your soul, and with all your strength" (Deut. 6:5). When you experience the love of God, you will love others. He will overcome you with His love as you experience His mighty visitation. Walking with Him is loving Him.

Chapter 19

Babel and the Day of Pentecost

Every day you are taught by the world how to walk in their
way. Now, we have been translated into the Kingdom of God
through Jesus Christ and the Holy Spirit teaches us how to
walk in His ways. The curse of Babylon has been broken.

The outpouring on the Day of Pentecost was a special day for all believers in Jerusalem. Jesus had told the disciples to wait for the promised Holy Spirit. "Behold, I send the Promise of My Father upon you; but tarry in the city of Jerusalem until you are *endued with power* from on high." (Luke 24:49)

The Holy Spirit would take His place as a Helper so that the disciples would not be left as orphans in this world (see John 14:18). He told them not to be afraid, that He would come to them. Jesus promised:

*But the Comforter (**Counselor, Helper, Intercessor, Advocate, Strengthener, Standby**), the Holy Spirit, Whom the Father will send in My name [in My place, to represent Me and act on My behalf], He will teach you all things. And He will cause you to recall* (will remind you of, bring to your remembrance) *everything I have told you. Peace I leave with you; My [own] peace I now give and bequeath to you. Not as the world gives do I give to you. Do not let your hearts be troubled, neither let them be afraid. [**Stop allowing yourselves to be agitated and disturbed; and do not permit yourselves to be fearful and intimidated and cowardly and unsettled**]* (John 14:26-27 AMPC).

This was an amazing time in history. *But it was meant for all believers everywhere until Jesus comes back.* I still look back on when Pentecost came into my life in the winter of 1980. I had just had my born-again experience with the Lord Jesus in the fall of that year—October sixth to be exact. I was on my way to work one snowy morning. We lived out in a rural area of Pennsylvania called New Kensington. I had been seeking the experience of the baptism of the Holy Spirit for a couple of months with no success. I did not understand that the Holy Spirit was not an experience but a person who loved me and wanted me to be filled with Him. I was not yielding to Him as a person. Because of this flaw in my belief system, I was just seeking the experience. The experience seemed to always be out of reach because I had not given myself over to walk with Him completely.

The roads were treacherous that morning, and I wondered if I could actually make it to work. It has to be really bad for me to turn around and go home because my family all learned to drive in these conditions ever since we started driving. I was getting closer to work when the falling snow became too much for me to see. Just then I began to slide into oncoming traffic. Just as I was about to collide with another car, I cried out to God in a loud voice with my eyes shut. I gave Him what He wanted. He wanted me to give Him the car. I loved that car more than Him. It is comical how when we are about to lose something, we are willing to turn that object over to God. I yelled out, "You can have my car." Immediately, I began speaking in tongues. The heavenly language flowed like a river, and I no longer could see anything because of the bright light in my car. My car and I were placed miraculously ahead on the road without even a scratch! I could never understand how those cars went through me on the highway without a trace. Thus began my powerful walk with Him in this life. When I was weak, He became strong. I know that this person called the Holy Spirit has changed my life. He helps me live and testify about Jesus.

If you do not know the Holy Spirit in this way, you need to ask Him to fill you. It is a subsequent experience to being born again. You will need this gift of power in your life. Having the Spirit in salvation and being filled with the Spirit are two entirely different events in a Christian's life. When I would get around other Christians, I would sense a unity that was supernatural. The Holy Spirit was bringing this unity among my new friends. I also noticed that my prayer language was bringing harmony to my life with God. When I would pray in the Spirit, I would sense oneness with God and His plan for me. Also, when I would pray in the Spirit with others, I would sense that same harmony spreading among us. What were we all saying in our heavenly languages, I wondered? Later, the Lord Jesus explained to me that Pentecost was the reversal of the curse at the tower of Babel!

Unity of the Faith

Behold, how good and how pleasant it is for brethren to dwell together in unity! (Psalm 133:1)

The story of Babel was told in the early chapters of the Book of Genesis. I was shown by the Lord that when the Spirit of God came to earth on the day of Pentecost, the Lord was reversing the curse that was implemented upon humanity because of their evil condition. Of course, the curse was only reversed on the believers who would receive the promised Holy Spirit. What the Lord showed me about this is located in the eleventh chapter of Genesis.

*Now the whole earth had one language and one speech. And it came to pass, as they journeyed from the east, that they found a plain in the land of Shinar, and they dwelt there. Then they said to one another, "Come, let us make bricks and bake them thoroughly." They had brick for stone, and they had asphalt for mortar. And they said, "Come, let us build ourselves a city, and a tower whose top is in the heavens; let us make a name for ourselves, lest we be scattered abroad over the face of the whole earth." But the Lord came down to see the city and the tower which the sons of men had built. And the Lord said, "**Indeed the people are one and they all have one language, and this is what they begin to do; now nothing that they propose to do will be withheld from them**. Come, let Us go down and there confuse their language, that they may not understand one another's speech." So the Lord scattered them abroad from there over the face of all the earth, and they ceased building the city. Therefore its name is called Babel, because there the Lord confused the language of all the earth; and from* *there the Lord scattered them abroad over the face of all the earth* (Genesis 11:1-9).

The Lord confused their language because the very intents of their heart were evil. Because of their unity, especially their ability to communicate, they were essentially able to accomplish anything that they set out to do in agreement with one another. The Lord saw that they would succeed at anything they put their hands to do. But being in their fallen, evil condition, the Lord could not allow them to continue.

You see, their hearts were wrong because of what they believed. Their ability to communicate meant that they would propagate their evil throughout the earth through communication and unity in their belief system. On the other hand, the outpouring on the day of Pentecost caused everyone who received the Holy Spirit to speak according to the Spirit, in a supernatural way, through a language that the individuals speaking did not know. Because of the belief system being the same among Christians, the harmony was there at its inception. They all were believing and thinking the same thing. Now, when we agree on anything, it is done for us in Heaven. This is a profound mystery concerning speaking and believing together in harmony. Unity must be established and maintained in the body of Christ. This is why satan fights unity so much. Satan *knows that we will get everything that we agree upon!*

The Lord gave us a government in the church that causes us to be built up and come into the unity of our faith. The apostle Paul understood this and instructed believers everywhere to allow God to govern us through the Spirit of God on us and through others who were appointed by God.

And He Himself gave some to be apostles, some prophets, some evangelists, and some pastors and teachers, for the equipping of the saints for the work of ministry, for the edifying of the body of Christ, till we all come to the unity of the faith and of the knowledge of the Son of God, to a perfect man, to the measure of the stature of the fullness of Christ; that we should no longer be children, tossed to and fro and carried about with every wind of doctrine, by the trickery of men, in the cunning craftiness of deceitful plotting, but, speaking the truth in love, may grow up in all things into Him who is the head—Christ—from whom the whole body, joined and knit together by what every joint supplies, according to the effective working by which every part does its share, causes growth of the body for the edifying of itself in love (Ephesians 4:11-16).

Remember what God said at Babel, "*Indeed the people are one and they all have one language, and this is what they begin to do; now nothing that they propose to do will be withheld from them.*" Compare this with the statement that Jesus said in the Book of Matthew:

Again I say to you that if two of you agree on earth concerning anything that they ask, it will be done for them by My Father in heaven. For where two or three are gathered together in My name, I am there in the midst of them (Matthew 18:19-20).

We can have answers to our prayers through agreement. We must contend for unity among ourselves. The apostle Paul said to the Ephesians, "endeavoring to keep the unity of the Spirit in the bond of peace" (Eph. 4:3).

Chapter 20

THE DEPTHS OF VISITATION AND PRAYER: THE STEPS JESUS WENT THROUGH IN HELL

I have set the Lord always before me; because He is at my right hand I shall not be moved. Therefore my heart is glad, and my glory rejoices; my flesh also will rest in hope. For You will not leave my soul in Sheol, nor will You allow Your Holy One to see corruption. You will show me the path of life; in Your presence is fullness of joy; at Your right hand are pleasures forevermore.
—PSALM 16:8-11

I love this passage of the Bible. Jesus knew it well as a young Jewish boy. He used it many times to remind Himself of the Father's love for Him and the deliverance from His enemies. He rehearsed scriptures such as this psalm. Jesus grew up in the stature and admonition of the Lord. As He grew in favor and wisdom, the plan of God was revealed in Scripture. His Father was the Holy Spirit, and He was preexistent before He came to the earth, so there was a lot inside of Him that was being unveiled as He grew up. As Jesus searched the Scriptures, He realized the truths that were there about Him, His purpose, and His destiny. His knowledge of those truths is the reason that He quoted a lot of the Old Testament. He discovered Himself in the Word, which gave Him the understanding that He was preordained. As He came closer to His death, burial, and resurrection, we know that He quoted Scripture concerning the events that were about to happen.

> *He endured torment and suffering for our salvation and our extremely successful life here on earth, especially in the area of prayer.*

One of the scriptures that He held on to tightly as He descended into the belly of the earth was a psalm. If you remember, when He was asked to come to pray for Lazarus, He waited until he had died before coming. In John, it says that He wept because He knew that He would be down there as well, for three days. He felt the compassion of the Father and the Holy Spirit as He said, "Lazarus, come forth." This was the same Spirit who raised Him from the dead. He was getting a preview of the process. That is why He wept. Jesus relinquished His authority, power, and His will over to the Father and the Holy Spirit. He commended His Spirit to them all as He descended into the pit. To fulfill all that was required by justice, He had to go further into hell than any man will ever have to go. He had to go to the depths of hell in order to make redemption complete. During those days in hell, He rehearsed Psalm 16 to Himself, believing that the Father would give the command for the Holy Spirit to raise Him to life again.

The Lord has taught me that it is from this place that He paved the way for us to pray from the depths of our spirit. Part of what Jesus obtained for us was this area of *deep intercession* and prayer. He has already been there for us, and so He has made it possible for us to pray from this area and receive complete deliverance and provision. It says in the book of James that the fervent prayer of a righteous man avails much (see James 5:16). Also, the apostle Paul says that the Spirit searches the deep things of God (see 1 Cor. 2:10). Jesus prayed from these depths, and He wants to teach us to pray from these depths as well.

> *If I were going to go to hell without Him, then He would have to go through everything down in hell for me to receive a complete salvation.*

The complete salvation that He accomplished allows me to pray to complete victory in any situation. There is no impossible situation with God, because He went to the depths for me already and it is my territory now. It belongs to me because He has given it to me. Not only can I pray myself out of hell's attacks, I can help others because the deliverance anointing is much more powerful than we know. We have this power available to us because of the things that Christ endured in hell for us. He rehearsed the psalm continually and was reminded of God's faithfulness to take Him out. The Holy Spirit showed Him the path of life back to this world and eventually the path to Heaven. He would not be left in Sheol. He would not see His body experience corruption or deterioration. Now, Jesus Christ assures me that nothing is impossible to me and that any enemy that confronts me is a defeated foe because every area of hell has been visited and conquered, every tormenting spirit has been overcome, and the Spirit of God has raised Jesus from the dead. That same Spirit has also raised me from the dead and quickened me in my body, my soul, my mind, my will, and my emotions.

Christ's journey into hell and resurrection has made my spirit a brand-new being (see 2 Cor. 5:17).

> *Jesus went through everything we go through so that we can have authority and victory in this life.*

One of things I have noticed, which is a result of this revelation of what Jesus went through, is the power of *command* that the Holy Spirit can implement in your life. As your spirit gets infused with His Spirit and the words that He has spoken become your words, the Holy Spirit comes in such a strong way that there is an authoritative command about you. That authority is something that reverberates, not only throughout this earth but also in hell. Demon spirits know that you have been infused with His Spirit and His Word and that His way of victory has become your reality. He has to turn over every place that Jesus tread. When you proclaim the Gospel, when you teach the people, and when you heal the sick and cast out devils and break the yokes, there is an authoritative command about you that is recognizable. You have become like Him on the earth. Greater things will you do because of the Holy Spirit's coming. The demons hear the voice of Jesus, they see the works of Jesus, and they therefore cannot stop any of what is said or done for God.

The Agreement

There is an agreement that the Trinity has concerning Jesus's life, death, burial, resurrection, and ascension to the right hand of God. Remember that Heaven is a timeless realm that would make this realm seem slow. Conversations occurred that were not recorded in the Bible. Jesus had an agreement with the Holy Spirit and with the Father about His activities from the time that He was born until the time that He ascended on high. Jesus submitted to the learning process and the disciplinary process that a normal Jewish boy would experience. We see this in the accounts of the Gospels. He did not start His ministry in power until the Holy Spirit came upon Him, just as any other person would have to do in order to fulfill their ministry on earth through the Holy Spirit. He said that everything that He did, He did because He saw the Father doing it. He said that everything He spoke, He spoke it because the Father spoke it. He then spoke by the Holy Spirit. He did not work independently of that guidance that was revealed by the Holy Spirit. This process was to fulfill all righteousness so that everything He went through in victory would be available to us.

Because Jesus fulfilled all righteousness, we are therefore able to have victory without having to master situations. Remember that Jesus went before us as our High Priest. He paved the way for us to be successful in everything. He did what He did in the earth realm, and it causes you to walk in such a visitation. During prayer, because of visitation you will see your prayers immediately answered. That is because you are walking in His authority, operating the way He did while He was here on the earth.

> *The Father and the Holy Spirit were not there in hell. Jesus says, "I'm going to relinquish My communication with Them so you don't have to go another day without Us."*

Jesus relinquished His communication with the Father and the Holy Spirit because He was thinking of us. We, at times, find ourselves in warfare. We may feel as though our communication has been cut off. It is at this point that we must rely solely on what Jesus did for us when He was in the belly of the earth. He told me that he rehearsed who He was and that He rehearsed the pl3an. He continued to do that until the Holy Spirit came and resurrected Him at the Father's command. If you feel as though you have been left alone and there is no communication between you and God or if you feel that your communication with Him only goes one way and He does not seem to answer you, just remember that this is the very time for your supernatural event to occur. That event will soon occur with your supernatural visitation because Jesus paved the way for you. He has already gone through the challenge of overcoming the situation. You will just have to rely on Him. You do not have to go another day without the Father, the Son, and Holy Spirit. You are now operating in visitation during prayer, and it is time to refuse to give up and stand planted in the Spirit.

Jesus relinquished His ability to deliver Himself, and He had to put total trust in the Father. He told me that this is the very secret that we must all learn—we must totally relinquish our ability to deliver ourselves and let God Himself coordinate our deliverance through the Holy Spirit. When you believe you cannot move forward anymore because an obstacle is in the way, you have to understand that this is an opportunity for you to experience a supernatural event. You are not to do anything to manipulate the situation in order to deliver yourself. You are to say, "Lord, You are my Deliverer and You will deliver me." You must submit to God, resist the devil, and he will flee from you.

"I had to go to the depths to suffer for you."

Jesus explained that the environment that He created for you for prayer is an environment that requires you to plumb the depths of your own heart and spirit. You must pray fervently in the spirit from a depth that can only be given to you by the Spirit of God Himself. Jesus explained the suffering that He went through for me in the depths of the belly of the earth. The Holy Spirit can take you to this place of intense prayer that Jesus prayed from the belly of the earth so that you experience the same victory of upending hell in your prayers. This victory over the enemy comes from that depth that He experienced for you. This is true intercession. The Holy Spirit will visit you and allow you to pray and intercede from this place where visitation becomes so powerful in the Spirit.

> *When you pray, remember Jesus says, "I did not see or feel the Father God in My suffering. I rehearsed who I was and I was delivered."*

Jesus explained to me that He had no witness from the Holy Spirit of who He was and His mission, only what was ingrained in His Spirit before being sent to the belly of the earth. The Holy Spirit was not there to witness to Him. The Father did not speak but turned His back on Him. In our lives, there are times when we also must stand strong in faith, believing for victory, even though it appears to not be coming forth. Jesus said in hard times you have to rehearse who you are and the scope of your mission because resurrection is surely coming. This is where the power of prayer is—in those moments when you feel nothing, you see nothing, you hear nothing, but the supernatural event of visitation is about to occur. Do not deliver yourself; trust in God, and He will do it.

> *He who calls you is faithful, who also will do it* (1 Thessalonians 5:24).

Therefore, if you feel like you are alienated from God or you cannot seem to find your way, start looking at the situation as though it is a platform that is prepared for you from which you will step into the supernatural. Then, when you comprehend the reality of the situation and the victory that Christ has already purchased, you will be able to believe in Him in a deeper way. He will not abandon you; He will bring you into victory. Start to pray from the depths of your spirit, and the same Spirit the rose Jesus from the dead will begin to pray through you. You will find not only a breakthrough in your life but a complete deluge of deliverance coming from Heaven. Remember Jesus down in the belly of the earth. He said that He was totally alienated from what He knew. There was no comfort or revelation there. He had to totally trust in the Father's plan, and so must we. We pray and know that we will be delivered. Do not be alarmed. Pray in the Holy Spirit, and God will resurrect you from this place of defeat to a place of overcoming victory. You will always receive the answers to your prayers from the depths of this place of surrender and humility.

> *"Everything was contrary to what I needed, and I didn't have the Holy Spirit for My comfort. I had to go through this for everyone."*

Chapter 21

PRAYER SECRETS

Jesus taught me how to pray effectively. He said to me, "Go to the depths as I did in prayer. If God does not deliver Me, then I will not be delivered. I rely on God, My Father, in prayer. He will deliver Me out of the depths with resurrection power!"

The Depths

Just as we discussed in the previous chapter, going to the depths as Jesus did in prayer is the first of the *prayer secrets*. You must pray from that *place of depth* where you say, just as Jesus said, *"If God doesn't deliver me, then I will not be delivered."*

And He was withdrawn from them about a stone's throw, and He knelt down and prayed, saying, "Father, if it is Your will, take this cup away from Me; nevertheless not My will, but Yours, be done." Then an angel appeared to Him from heaven, strengthening Him. And being in agony, He prayed more earnestly. Then His sweat became like great drops of blood falling down to the ground (Luke 22:41-44).

"The depths" is a place where there is complete surrender and, as Moses said, "If You do not go with us, we're not going" (see Exod. 33:15). You must resolve that God Himself is your only way out, and you must choose not to deliver yourself by manipulating. You must refuse to rely upon any crutches in your life that need to be thrown away. Then, and only then, you will see God show up in your situation. You are going to have visitation in prayer. Just tell the devil that you will not bow to him but that God, whom you rely on continually, will answer with resurrection power! The apostle Paul said, "And the Lord will *deliver me* from every evil work and preserve me for His heavenly kingdom. To Him be glory forever and ever. Amen!" (2 Tim. 4:18).

> *Allow God to be bigger than the checkbook, credit card, any person, or any circumstance! He is bigger! He knew what your challenges in life were going to be.*

Whatever it is that is presenting itself to you as being bigger than God, you tell it that it must bow before the God of the universe. Because God knew what you were going to go through already, He has provided a way of escape for you so that you can bear up under it (see 1 Cor. 10:13). So wait on the Lord and let Him be your strength. He will deliver you.

> *"Nevertheless, Father, not My will but Yours." He relinquished His own will. From this same position that Christ created, you pray. It is a position that is from the depths of God! From this position you say, "If You do not go with me, I am not going."*

Relinquish Your Will

Let us talk a little about the atmosphere around you that Heaven has provided. This atmosphere is not from the earthly realm but is created by the Holy Spirit. The Holy Spirit has been called alongside you to help you (see John 14:26). He will "teach you all things" about this atmosphere of Heaven. He will reside inside you.

The second of the *prayer secrets* is to *relinquish your will to the Holy One*. This comes as the Holy One cultivates your environment around you as well as within you to create a place where the Trinity will come and dwell. Relinquishing your will comes as you fall in love with Him and He illuminates you in a holy fire. You find yourself being captured by His power and doing His will as all things become clear to you. Jesus replied, "All who love me will do what I say. My Father will love them, and we will come and make our home with each of them" (John 14:23 NLT).

> *David was a man after God's heart. You are to be as passionate!*

Holy Passion

I thirst for God, the living God. When can I go and stand before him? (Psalm 42:2 NLT)

One of the things you will realize as you yield to the Holy Spirit is that He will give you a passion to seek after God in holiness. *Holy passion is part of the baptism of fire* and the third of the *prayer secrets*. The Holy One's fire cleanses you and also causes you to see Him in a greater way. In the letter to the Corinthians, the apostle Paul says that no one knows the heart of God except the Spirit of God. Through visitation of the Spirit, we receive revelation and obtain the mind of God through Jesus Christ. We know that the Spirit of God will seek out the depths of God (see 1 Cor. 2:10-12).

David sought after God. When you seek Him with all your heart, you will be rewarded. He is a Rewarder of those who diligently seek Him (see Heb. 11:6). If you notice, we all seem to have things about which we are passionate. As long as it is not just the fleshly nature, we can pursue those things because they are part of our creative gifts and talents. At the same time, we should start to allow our passion to grow for God and to see His glory. When we seek Him first, all the "other things" shall be added unto us (see Matt. 6:33). David was a man after God's heart:

> *And when he had removed him, he raised up unto them David to be their king; to whom also he gave their testimony, and said, I have found David the son of Jesse, a man after mine own heart, which shall fulfil all my will* (Acts 13:22 KJV).

Pray from the depth that only the Spirit in your spirit knows.

The Spirit Knows

As we mentioned earlier, the *Holy Spirit knows the heart of God*, our Father. When we trust Him to reveal the Father's heart to us, we enter into *the fourth of the prayer secrets—waiting on the Holy Spirit.* He knows! This secret is little known or practiced because our culture is one that requires us to be busy and in a hurry all day long. Little time is taken to be still and know that He is God. The Spirit knows God's will and wants to communicate that to us. The apostle Paul said it this way:

> *And in a similar way, the Holy Spirit takes hold of us in our human frailty to empower us in our weakness. For example, at times we don't even know how to pray, or know the best things to ask. However, the Holy Spirit rises up within us to super-intercede on our behalf, pleading to God with emotional sighs too deep for words. God, the searcher of the heart, knows fully our longings, yet he also understands the desires of the Spirit, because the Holy Spirit passionately pleads before God for us, his holy ones, in perfect harmony with God's plan and our destiny (Romans 8:26-27 TPT).*

> *Jesus taught me in my heavenly visitation that the single most important thing I could do to participate in the supernatural realm was to pray in tongues.*

Pray in Tongues

The fifth of the *prayer secrets* is *praying in tongues.* Sometimes we do not have the ability to pray effectively because of our limitations. I always encourage people to know what their limitations are and yield to the "Greater One" within them. If you do not know how you should pray in any situation, yield to the Holy Spirit and to the baptism of the Holy Spirit. "Likewise the Spirit also helps in our weaknesses. For we do not know what we should pray for as we ought, but the Spirit Himself makes intercession for us with groanings which cannot be uttered"

(Rom. 8:26). The Holy Spirit has been given as a friend, a standby to help you pray in any situation. He will give you words to speak that are not in your language. However, those words are going directly to God and asking for the correct thing automatically.

When you yield to the Holy Spirit in this way and speak in other tongues, you cannot utter a wrong prayer. Praying in tongues is the perfect prayer. It is free, and it has already been given. All you need to do is to take care and not lean on your own understanding and yield to the greater One within you. He knows how to pray for you and get the job done. Our enemy fights this more than anything because he knows he cannot win against people who will allow the Holy Spirit to pray through them. That should tell you something about yielding and letting the Holy One pray through you. The apostle Paul said:

> *When someone speaks in tongues, no one understands a word he says, because he's not speaking to people, but to God—he is speaking intimate mysteries in the Spirit. But when someone prophesies, he speaks to encourage people, to build them up, and to bring them comfort. The one who speaks in tongues advances his own spiritual progress, while the one who prophesies builds up the church* (1 Corinthians 14:2-4 TPT).

So go ahead and speak by the power of God and let your destiny and purpose be prayed out and spoken into existence.

Partake in His Sufferings

Part of what *prayer during visitation* does is address the discrepancies that we encounter in this earthly realm. Our daily life on this earth is filled with situations that do not match the heavenly realm and the Word of God. We constantly have to bring correction through our actions, words, and prayer. This is part of the process of implementing truth into our daily lives. The revelation that the Spirit brings in heavenly visitation causes us to speak out the truth in prayer even if it does not appear to match the facts. Many of the things we go through during our day are warfare that the enemy is bringing against us because we stand for truth. Satan confronts us because he does not want us to gain any momentum in this earthly realm; we gain momentum by agreeing with God, so satan does all he can do to prevent our agreement with the Lord. By praying successfully through spiritual warfare during visitation and getting other people to be on the same page as well, we will bring strength because of unity. Finally, when agreeing corporately we are bringing the Kingdom of God into manifestation in this earthly realm.

The minute that you receive the Word of God with joy, satan comes to steal that Word before it can take root. Every time that you hear from God, every time you are encouraged, every time that you walk in the will and purpose of God, you are going to have to stand for truth. You might have to suffer as a result. You might as well get ready because your victory is imminent as long as you are prepared for battle. Part of that battle means that you may suffer for doing good and trusting in God. "But when you do good and suffer, if you take it patiently, this is commendable before God" (1 Pet. 2:20).

> ## *"You are going to suffer for Me."*

This chapter is to encourage you that this process of suffering for Him is a good process. This process helps you to distinguish where your limitations are and where you need to turn over your weaknesses to Him so that they can become strengths. There are great rewards for suffering for Jesus Christ. Do not be disappointed if you have opportunity to suffer; it is a part of the process here on earth. Jesus had to suffer while He was here, and so do we. Because of the sinful discrepancies between the earthly and heavenly realms, we will suffer. "Yes, and all who desire to live godly in Christ Jesus will suffer persecution" (2 Tim. 3:12). Let us hear what is being said here and resolve this forever. Suffering for what is the truth will always be part of our life as Christians. But remember what Jesus said, "These things I have spoken to you, that in Me you may have peace. In the world you will have tribulation; but be of good cheer, I have overcome the world" (John 16:33).

When you count the cost of following Him and humbly accept the fact that you are not accepted by the world, then the Lord accepts you. You may have to walk away from people, places, and things to follow Jesus completely. Do not let that bother you. He predicted the suffering and persecution for His sake.

> So Jesus answered and said, "Assuredly, I say to you, there is no one who has left house or brothers or sisters or father or mother or wife or children or lands, for My sake and the gospel's, who shall not receive a hundredfold now in this time—houses and brothers and sisters and mothers and children and lands, **with persecutions**—and in the age to come, eternal life. But many who are first will be last, and the last first" (Mark 10:29-31).

If you want to receive a hundredfold now in this time—houses and brothers and sisters and mothers and children and lands—then you will have persecution as well. You will have to die to yourself to have a resurrection.

> *"Your identity is with Me. Come to the end of yourself; die to yourself."*

Your Identity in Visitation

Just think of Jesus being the answer to all of your prayers. There is not one request that He does not want to answer. As you walk with Him, He will influence you to change. You will start to desire to be more like Him, and your prayer life is going to change. You realize that in a relationship with Him, you do not have to twist His arm; you just need talk to Him. When you desire to be in a relationship with someone, you want the relationship to be about who they are, not what they can do for you. Jesus desires a relationship with you. When you seek Him for who He is and not what He can do for you, then He will answer your prayers because you trust Him. Most people know that God can do something to answer their prayers but do not realize that He is willing to answer prayers as well because of who He is. Knowing the ways of God is greater than knowing His acts (see Ps. 103:7). He is willing, but you may not be walking with Him in visitation. If you do not have that visitation with Jesus, your prayers may go unanswered. Being alone with Jesus at times can be good because it helps you to spend time cultivating your relationship with God. When you learn not to try to preserve yourself in suffering but let Him have you completely, your prayers will start to be answered.

Often, your prayers have the status of "pending." I see your status in "signs" above you. Because of self-preservation, your prayers are not going any further. You need the new sign "processed" or "delivered" over your head. You need to yield to what Jesus is saying here, and then you will have your prayers answered.

A Sacrifice That Counts

The Lord reminded me of this truth, "You cannot have resurrection without death." He said, "Unless a grain of wheat falls into the ground and *dies*, it remains alone; but if it *dies*, it produces much grain. He who loves his life will lose it, and he who hates his life in this world will keep it for eternal life" (John 12:24-25). I found that after I died to my fleshly desires, God accepted me into a new realm. It is a fabulous realm of Heaven where I always receive the answers to my prayers.

> *Let resurrection power flow. Many people have sacrificed to be here. Your reward is based on what it cost you to be in this miracle flow of resurrection power.*

Part of what we experience during prayer is what Jesus encountered when He prayed. He was suffering at times, and yet He was able to give the ultimate sacrifice. In prayer, God visited Him so that He could relinquish His own will in any situation and submit to Heaven's wishes. Jesus prayed, "Father, if it is Your will, take this cup away from Me; nevertheless not My will, but Yours, be done" (Luke 22:42).

I found that we can experience resurrection power when we die to ourselves in prayer. We will find ourselves quickened by the Holy One, and prayer becomes an extraordinary experience that will put us into a dominant place over the enemy. This is accomplished by imitating Jesus in the way that He relinquished His will, died to what He wanted, and yielded to the Father.

> *What is it that is so dear to you it prevents you from coming and allowing the Spirit of God to have preeminence over you?*

Please do not be afraid of what God has prepared for you. He will give far better answers to prayer than you could possibly ever think or imagine. You just have to trust Him to reveal what He has for you by His Spirit, and then you will see it come to pass. *Nothing* should be so dear to you that you cannot let go of it. When you release those things that seems so difficult to release, you will see the Holy Spirit completely surprise you with His ability to bless you beyond what you could ever possibly ask, think, or imagine.

I am so amazed that there are no disappointments in Heaven. In God's perfect Kingdom of Heaven, there is absolutely no instance where everything does not work out perfectly. In the Kingdom of Heaven, everything that is appointed to happen does appear, and you do not miss your appointments. Everything that you pray is heard, and if you pray with the power of the Holy Spirit and His revelation, you will have it. I find that I cannot lose when He is there with me, helping me pray into my appointments. The Spirit does not ever know defeat. He laughs at the devil all the time. Why not do the same as you yield your whole being to Him? He is your *everything*, and He will only lead you into your appointments. "For in Him we live and move and have our being" (Acts 17:28). It is time to yield and be healed of past traumas. Your prayers are pending, and you need complete healing.

> *In God, there are no disappointments, just appointments.*

Pray from the depths of your heart. All the answers to prayers that are pending are about to arrive. Your prayers may be held back by the same type of trauma that satan brought against you in previous situations. It is trauma, and it is not your fault. Be healed!

God has destined you for success in His Kingdom. Doing His perfect will in your life is His first and foremost desire for you. He wants to bless you with His presence and answer your prayers. Trauma left over from satan's attacks can hinder you and prevent you from entering the *visitation in prayer* realm.

I want you to be healed of all the damage that satan may have performed in your life, and so does the Lord. We must take authority over him in the name of Jesus. He no longer can attack you when you confront him in the name of Jesus. After we break his power over you, we must drive him out and forbid him to come back. Finally, we must receive healing in the name of Jesus for any damage done to us in our mind, will, and emotions.

Jesus, by the Holy Spirit, will search the deep parts of you. He will look for any area of your house that is occupied with anything that is not of Him. He wants you to be healed. He will want to take anything that is not of Him and move it out so He can inhabit your innermost being fully. This process can be painful as you realize that you are taking out things in you that were once idols upon which you depended. The hurts that you experienced in your past have also caused you to go into survival mode. This mode does not allow you to function effectively in the activities of the Holy Spirit. It causes you to be in cycles where you become a continual victim and orphan instead of God's child.

> *God says, "I even want to go to the very depths of your being. Whatever you vacate, I will fill your innermost being with Myself."*

When God comes in and asks you to give Him areas that are inside of you that no one is allowed to access, His goal is for you to live and move and have your being *in Him*. Because of His habitation within your innermost being, He will ask for access to your basement—the deepest part of your being—because He wants to give you everything He has. He wants to heal every hurt within your being. He knows that your prayer life needs visitation.

The God, Who produced and formed the world and all things in it, being Lord of heaven and earth, does not dwell in handmade shrines. Neither is He served by human hands, as though He lacked anything, for it is He Himself Who gives life and breath and all things to all [people]. And He made from one [common origin, one source, one blood] all nations of men to settle on the face of the earth, having definitely determined [their] allotted periods of time and the fixed boundaries of their habitation (their settlements, lands, and abodes), *so that they should seek God,* **in the hope that they might feel after Him and find Him, although He is not far from each one of us. For in Him we live and move and have our being;** *as even some of your [own] poets have said, for we are also His offspring. Since then we are God's offspring, we ought not to suppose that Deity* (the Godhead) *is like gold or silver or stone, [of the nature of] a representation by human art and imagination, or anything constructed or invented. Such [former] ages of ignorance God, it is true, ignored and allowed to pass unnoticed; but now He charges all people everywhere to repent* (to change their minds for the better and heartily to amend their ways, with abhorrence of their past sins), *because He has fixed a day when He will judge the world righteously* (justly) *by a Man Whom He has destined and appointed for that task, and He has made this credible and given conviction and assurance and evidence to everyone by raising Him from the dead* (Acts 17:24-31 AMPC).

Why does it sometimes seem impossible for people get their prayers answered? Jesus explained to me that the answer to that question is in Matthew 13. You cannot get a crop out of what you did not sow. You cannot access something you do not know about. You must receive the Word in good ground. It will produce a crop, and your prayers will be answered according to the word that was sown in you. You will hear, see, and receive.

We all need to learn the principles contained in this parable. Why? Because Jesus said, "You've been given the intimate experience of insight into the hidden truths and mysteries of the reign of heaven's kingdom, but they have not" (Matt. 13:11 TPT). This is similar to the statement that the apostle Paul made. In the letter to the Corinthian church concerning the ministry of the Holy Spirit, Paul states that the Spirit of God brings forth the "deep things of God" (1 Cor. 2:10). There are mysteries that need to be revealed, and we can be the recipients of those mysteries!

Jesus went on to explain the parable:

> For everyone who listens with an open heart will receive progressively more revelation until he has more than enough. But those who don't listen with an open, teachable heart, even the understanding that they think they have will be taken from them. That is why I teach the people using parables, because they think they're looking for truth, yet because their hearts are unteachable, they never discover it. Although they will listen to me, they never fully perceive the message I speak (1 Corinthians 13:12-13 TPT).

There are *prayer secrets* in this parable. First, we must tend to our "ground" so that it produces a crop. In reviewing the types of ground in Chapter 2, I want you to see the words I highlighted in bold letters.

The Footpath

- They do not understand it.
- The evil one comes and snatches away the seed.

The Rocky Soil

- They fall away.

- They have problems.

- They are persecuted for believing God's Word.

The Thorns

- They hear God's Word.

- The message is crowded out by the worries of this life and the lure of wealth.

- No fruit is produced.

The Good Soil

- They truly hear and understand.

- God's Word produces a harvest.

- The results are then thirty, sixty, or even a hundred times as much as had been planted!

We tend to our ground by getting it ready for planting and receiving a good harvest. Be diligent with the removal of everything that Jesus has told you is a hindrance to your soil. The Spirit will help you to sort through those challenges and resolve all issues. Because of the process of preparing your soil, your prayers will begin to be answered because you are then free to pray into the perfect will of God. You will see a harvest of the Word come forth, thirty, sixty, or even a hundred times more than planted.

Second, we must realize that this is not just the parable of the *sower*. This is actually the parable of the *soil*. The seed does its job according to what is inherent in it. The soil is the determining factor. So the deep mystery of the Kingdom being given to you requires that you prepare the soil by dealing with its issues. When you address these issues, then you will see a harvest.

In our lives, we need to deal with these "soil" issues immediately. I have listed those things we must adjust so that our prayers are not hindered. Jesus went over these with His disciples, so these hindrances must be important to overcome.

These are the deep mysteries of the Kingdom that must be unveiled to us in order to encounter abundance in our life. Our prayer life will increase supernaturally after implementing these secrets into our lives:

- **Whatever we do not understand** must be understood. Therefore, to gain understanding, we are to pray for it. We also must be aware that the evil one will attempt immediately to come and steal the Word from you to prevent you from receiving that which God intended for you to receive.

- **When we have problems**, we need to seek help from the Lord immediately *so that we do not fall away*. We need to have a group of believers who will receive us when we get persecuted because of the Word of God. There are churches and gatherings where we can go and receive help and strength.

- **We need to remember that worry can sometimes become too much of a focus in life** and can then become preeminent and push the Word of God out. The Word can be crowded out by worries of this life or seduction of wealth. The lack of the Word can cause no fruit to be produced. We must guard against this and not tolerate worry or wealth to seduce us.

- **Remember, when we truly hear and understand** what God is saying, we will have a harvest. It will be much more than what we planted. The mysteries of the Kingdom have been revealed through this parable. The secret is this: "If you are not obtaining your crop, there is something wrong with the soil, not the seed."

These are the deep secrets of the Kingdom. It is the *parable of the soil*. I pray by the Holy Spirit that you receive healing, deliverance, and restoration now, in the mighty name of Jesus. Holy Spirit, help us get our soil ready for a harvest. I want fruit that lasts. I want everyone to come in!

When you give your life to the Lord, it is for your benefit in so many ways. The Spirit of God can take what you give Him and make it beautiful. You would never want to pay the price for something and not receive that particular item. You also would not want to receive an item only to discover that the item was not worth the cost that you paid. Well, giving your life to the Lord is not only worth it, it is permanent. That is what is in every gift God gives us—the potential to be permanent. We produce fruit by being connected to Him and His fruit is permanent. We are not going to fade away. We are going to produce fruit that continues to grow and reproduce at all the times!

Relationship Discrepancies

One of the most powerful revelations I received from Jesus was the fact that we need to be transparent and humble before Him. When we allow the Holy Spirit to mentor us, we become attractive to Heaven relationally and not just positionally. Many of us depend on our positional rights exclusively. He desires to dwell with you, and that in itself will transform your prayer life! However, because of the fact that there are character issues within us that need to be resolved, we will grieve the Holy Spirit as long as we remain unhealed. We desperately need the Holy Spirit to heal any emotional wounds from trauma that we have encountered from the enemy. Being in the state of trauma can cause demonic attacks. The demons will always try to take advantage of your weaknesses and keep you out of the faith realm. If you are out of the faith realm, then you cannot expect to get your prayers answered. The apostle John said:

> But when you ask him, be sure that your faith is in God alone. Do not waver, for a person with divided loyalty is as unsettled as a wave of the sea that is blown and tossed by the wind. Such people should not expect to receive anything from the Lord. **Their loyalty is divided between God and the world, and they are unstable in everything they do** (James 1:6-8 NLT).

The reason we are not getting prayers answered is because there are discrepancies in our relationship with Him.

Holy Conviction

We need to let the Holy Spirit work in our lives. He is the perfect representation of God the Father and His character. When He shows up, He passes on the character of God the Father to the world whether they know Him or not. He automatically convicts the world of sin, righteousness, and judgment. According to Scripture, the one important aspect of the Holy Spirit's work in the earth is judgment (see John 16:8-11). This ministry of convicting the world concerning judgment is because the ruler of this world, the devil, is judged. This is why anyone under the devil's rule is going to the same place that he is going—hell. So if you are a Christian, you are delivered and must enforce your position daily. You must compel others to come out of the world and be reconciled to God through Jesus Christ. The devil cannot touch you. He should be afraid of you. He knows those who do not have this understanding of their power and authority over him, so he still readily attacks them. Let the Holy Spirit teach you these concepts, and yield to the holy fire in you prayer life! It will bring you victory.

> *The Holy Spirit convicts concerning sin, righteousness, and judgment. If satan has been judged, why is he still bothering you?*

Put Your Foot Down

Here is one of the biggest mysteries to be revealed in your prayer life—the believer's authority in Jesus Christ. Jesus has let me know that we have been given authority. Listen to what Jesus said to the disciples:

> *Then the seventy returned with joy, saying, "Lord, even **the demons are subject to us in Your name**." And He said to them, "I saw Satan fall like lightning from heaven. Behold, **I give you the authority** to trample on serpents and scorpions, and over all the power of the enemy, and nothing shall by any means hurt you. Nevertheless do not rejoice in this, that the spirits are subject to you, but rather rejoice because your names are written in heaven" (Luke 10:17-20).*

The main reason for highlighting the importance of our authority as believers is that you must know that you are now responsible for trampling on the enemy and driving him away; he cannot touch you. So why is he still bothering you?

First, you have to be thoroughly convinced by the revelation of the Spirit concerning the Word of God. The devil knows that if you have an authoritative command about you emanating from your very being, you will speak as one of God's generals! And he knows he then must obey your authority.

Second, if we will relentlessly drive him out, he will suffer so much harm that he cannot afford to return because of the total defeat that he will encounter. You must continue to enforce your position against him at all times.

Third, you must remember that you will be effective in all you will attempt because you have been adopted into the family of Heaven. Your name is written there. When you encounter the enemy, remember that it is He who is with you whom you represent that renders you totally and victoriously effective! He is Jesus Christ; He is Lord of all.

> *If satan is still bothering you, it is strictly your*
> *responsibility to do something about it!*

Chapter 22

LOOKING AT YOUR DESTINY

Your Focus

Your destiny is just as important to God your Father as it is to you. There are so many intricacies that are written in your books that the Kingdom of Heaven must coordinate from the conference room. It is a command center in Heaven. Jesus has so much invested in you as a person that what is written about you has become one of His highest priorities. The secret is that your destiny is tied not only to Heaven, but also to the many people you will influence on earth. The people you will affect have already been named before eternity. They are listed in writing in your books in Heaven.

> *While people are looking at their performance,*
> *I am looking at my target—Jesus!*

If you sense your destiny at this moment, remember that sometimes we become so performance-oriented that it hinders our effectiveness for God. It takes the joy away from serving God. If you really want to look and focus on your goal, Jesus should be the one upon whom you look. He is the Author and Finisher of our faith. The book of Hebrews says:

> Therefore we also, since we are surrounded by so great a cloud of witnesses, let us lay aside every weight, and the sin which so easily ensnares us, and let us **run with endurance the race that is set before us, looking unto Jesus, the author and finisher of our faith**, who for the joy that was set before Him endured the cross, despising the shame, and has sat down at the right hand of the throne of God (Hebrews 12:1-2).

Remember, when we pray we should always set Jesus before us. He is our one and only goal. King David said, "I have set the Lord always before me; because He is at my right hand I shall not be moved" (Ps. 16:8). When we set Jesus before ourselves in prayer, we will not be moved in our faith. The steadfastness that then arises will create an environment of destiny around us as we stand in immovable faith. We will then see our prayers answered completely.

When you focus on King Jesus, He will begin to focus on you. When the Almighty focuses on you, things are going to start happening quickly. He will desire to bless you far beyond what you can possibly imagine. You will be in favor with Him. God will start to reveal His intentions for you. He will stand on your destiny and prepare that destiny for you. God has wonderful plans. He is excited about those plans. However, you must yield to Him. You must set your heart on pleasing Him.

God says to you, "I want to reveal My intentions for you."

Not Performance

Performance is a big concern in our corporate culture. Your success is based on data that is gathered to prove how well you are doing any given task. You are in competition many times with others. The competition can even include historical data of those who went before you. The Kingdom of God concerns these three elements—righteousness, peace, and joy in the Holy Spirit (see Rom. 14:17). These are the characteristics of the Kingdom that involved us. I want to emphasize that our goal is to *attain Him* as the apostle Paul did. He said:

> *I don't mean to say that I have already achieved these things or that I have already reached perfection. But I press on to possess that perfection for which Christ Jesus first possessed me. No, dear brothers and sisters, I have not achieved it, but **I focus on this one thing: Forgetting the past and looking forward to what lies ahead, I press on to reach the end of the race and receive the heavenly prize for which God, through Christ Jesus, is calling us*** (Philippians 3:12-14 NLT).

God asks all of us, "Where are you going?" Your life is not based on your performance like the corporate culture that focuses on performance data. Your life is based upon achieving the goal of gaining Him, which comes from losing your life so you may gain what He has for you, which will be far better than what you have forfeited.

How do we please God? We please God by focusing on Jesus and making Him our goal. He showed me that He will stand on your destiny and ask you to come to Him. When you seek Him, the Holy Spirit will guide you into all truth and put you in your perfect destiny that Jesus desires for you to obtain! What more could you ask? He sets it up so that you will have a wonderful walk with Him to your destiny.

When you arrive, you will be so blessed to know that any price that you had to pay was worth it. You will see that along the way you were being groomed for leadership in eternity with Him. You learned how to pray effectively. You also learned how to walk in your authority.

> *Jesus is standing at your destiny, and He*
> *is asking you to come to Him.*

Authorized for a Purpose

When praying, remember that your destiny gives you supernatural access to miracles. That is correct, I said *miracles!* God is on your side. He already wants to answer your prayers. This is the truth about your walk with Him. "But if *we walk in the light as He is in the light*, we have fellowship with one another, and the blood of Jesus Christ His Son cleanses us from all sin" (1 John 1:7).

So the first concept to understand is that Jesus desires to walk with you the whole way in the light of Heaven and in the presence of God Himself. He has authorized your purpose. Second, because He is the Author and Creator of your destiny, you can be assured that He will help you to fulfill and finish your destiny in a beautiful way. Third, because of the commitment that you make to walk with Him, He will always be committed to you. He will ensure that you arrive at your destiny. This is why we must move toward Him and pray the whole way—because *He hears us.*

> *Now this is the confidence that we have in Him, that if we ask anything according to His will, He hears us. And if we know that **He hears us, whatever we ask, we know that we have the petitions that we have asked of Him** (1 John 5:14-15).*

Last, God has a high calling on your life. That calling is so important to God and to any other person you may have been assigned by Heaven to assist. He is the Most High, and His calling on your life is a "high" calling. So, continue to progress toward Jesus and focus upon what He has for you. Prayer is communication. Prayer is a vital part of your walk toward your destiny (see Phil. 3:12).

> *Jesus authorized your purpose. He will finish and complete it. I will commit that which I have; I go toward the high calling.*

What Is Next

The Holy Spirit always wants to help us understand some truth that is a mystery to us. We obviously do not know everything. The Holy One always wants to reveal Jesus to us. When we pray, He comes alongside us as a Counselor to coach us on every detail that we may require. It may be in an unknown tongue that He gives us to pray out those details. He will coach you with such accuracy, fervency, and passion that it will take you into the Father's perfect will. Father God is so pleased when we trust His Spirit. We will then be walking with Jesus and encountering answered prayer.

If you want all of your prayers answered, you will find that they are answered when you walk in complete unity with Jesus. The Holy Spirit is a person. He was sent from God. He acts as our Counselor. He coaches us!

The Realms of God

The realms of God are so much higher than ours. The Father has given us the mighty Holy Spirit to escort us into this realm. The realms of God's Kingdom create the environment of Heaven. If the Spirit of God takes you into the realms of Heaven to pray, faith will arise as you learn to live by His ways and not your own. Prayer is answered because you are in perfect faith with Him. Your faith must prevail and eliminate all doubt. The Holy Spirit then will encounter no hindrance when He is dealing with you. He will be able to be so convincing when He helps you to understand these critical essentials to answered prayer. He requires nothing from you except your yielded life and obedience.

Allowing the Counselor to take you into "prayer conquests" is really a preparation that sets you up for answered prayer. Jesus said, "Prove by the way you live that you have repented of your sins and turned to God" (Matt. 3:8 NLT).

By repentance, you have chosen to walk with Him fully, leaving your old life. To some Christians, this is in the fine print of the contract that they have failed to read. You made a covenant with God when you became born again of the Spirit. By leaving your old life, you are free to do whatever the Spirit is saying to you. He is the Holy One. He will put you right into the middle of truth. Then, you are free to pray out the mysteries of God, unhindered by the flesh and your old life because He has set you free. "So if the Son sets you free, you are truly free" (John 8:36 NLT).

> *If only you would let Him take you up into His realm and let Him pray with you and through you!*

Guardian Angels

Angels are with you because they have a vital part in your destiny. The books that are written about your days on earth are available to be read and enforced by these wonderful servants of God. Psalms clearly speaks about your destiny written in a book. "You saw me before I was born. Every day of my life was recorded in your book. Every moment was laid out before a single day had passed" (Ps. 139:16 NLT).

Angels are "ministering spirits sent forth to minister for those who will inherit salvation" (Heb. 1:14). These angels love to perform God's will and they understand God's plan for you. Angels are constantly listening and ready to do the will of our Father God. "Bless the Lord, you His angels, who excel in strength, who do His word, heeding the voice of His word" (Ps. 103:20).

Angels are assigned to you when you are a little child. They remain ever with you as you grow up. You do not lose your angel just because you got older! Most of us need angels now more than ever!

> *Take heed that you do not despise one of these **little ones,** for I say to you that in heaven **their angels always see the face of My Father who is in heaven** (Matthew 18:10).*

> ### Your guardian angels were sent from God. They have been sent only for you! Angels do not age.

The angels love it when your prayers are in complete agreement with the will of Father God. When you pray by the Holy Spirit, the angels will recognize that fact; they will harken unto the voice of the Lord as you speak by the Spirit. They already know what God says and will not accept *no* for an answer. They answer the prayers that are born of the Spirit. This is very important. You must be full of the Holy Spirit and speak by the Spirit. He wants to lead you into all truth. Always rely on the written Word of God and speak it out. Angels only harken to what He has already said and what He is saying by the Spirit now. What God has said and what the Spirit speaks now always are completely in agreement. God will reward my angels for their faithfulness. They get to see and worship the Almighty all the time. They feel privileged to help us succeed and reach our destiny.

> *I am spending eternity with Jesus, and my angels*
> *have the privilege of helping me to succeed.*

Heaven's Intent

We live in a time that will culminate all the other moves and produce a finale like no other in His presence. As we approach the time of transition into the Kingdom's reign on earth, we will see many events that pertain to prophecy. Satan understands only as much as God will allow him to understand. He is in the dark about the timing of future events. He is not allowed to take over the earth yet because the church is still on the earth as the bride of Christ. Certain things are set in stone. We must allow the mighty angels and the Spirit of God to begin to coordinate this next move of the Spirit. That move of the Spirit will soon be upon us. Heaven wants us to succeed. But everyone in Heaven comprehends the fact that we must be full of understanding and that we must have the Holy Spirit fire to move forward with this victory.

> *Every intent of Heaven is for me is to succeed.*
> *Soon, the powers of the coming age will be here!*
> *Let us be ready for the millennial reign.*

Eyes That See

The apostle Paul prayed for the Ephesians to have their eyes enlightened that they may see (see Eph. 1:17-23). The Holy Spirit is the One who reveals truth to you. There is no one who wants to help you as He does. Jesus wants us to begin to speak out His words into the earth realm. He wants us to start seeing into the Spirit realm. Words are a very important part of prayer. Jesus said:

> It is the Spirit Who gives life [He is the Life-giver]; the flesh conveys no benefit whatever [there is no profit in it]. **The words (truths) that I have been speaking to you are spirit and life** (John 6:63 AMPC).

Let us allow the life of Jesus to come out of our mouths in the form of words. Also, let us yield to the Spirit and have the manifest presence of God in our lives. Then let us release that presence out into the environment. Always remember to keep this foremost in your mind—the same power that rose Jesus from the dead will give life to your mortal body (see Rom. 8:11).

> *I need eyes that really see into the realm of the Spirit. I have sight through Jesus Christ! His words are Spirit and they are life. Everything that emanates from Him is life flowing into my flesh and quickening me.*

Enter In

The Lord is asking us to walk through those doors that He has destined for us. The apostle Paul said, "For a great and *effective door has opened* to me, and there are many adversaries" (1 Cor. 16:8-9). Paul saw that there were doors that were *effective*. What door is God asking you to step through that He has opened just for you?

Even if you do not know the specifics of these doors, you can know for sure is that there is always the one door we need to go through all the time. He is called *the Door*. Jesus said

*Most assuredly, I say to you, I am **the door** of the sheep. All who ever came before Me are thieves and robbers, but the sheep did not hear them. I am the door. If anyone enters by Me, he will be saved, and will go in and out and find pasture. The thief does not come except to steal, and to kill, and to destroy. I have come that they may have life, and that they may have it more abundantly* (John 10:7-10).

We can focus upon Jesus as the Door until the Holy Spirit reveals the other doors that you are to walk through. Heaven is waiting. Everyone and every being in Heaven wants to help you pray and receive your destiny.

The apostle Paul was able to discern the door in the Spirit, and we should enter in through those doors when the Spirit shows them to us. This will happen in times of prayer. The Holy Spirit will open our eyes and ask us to enter in.

> *Enter in now; there are no angels in Heaven that are standing without performing a purpose. They are ready to help you implement the will of God in the earth. This includes a mighty move of the Spirit as people come into their destinies.*

Once you enter in, you can have so much of Heaven happening inside of you that the heaven within you desires to spring forth and manifest itself wherever you may be! You will feel your prayers turn into intercession. You will be interceding for the move of the Spirit in your midst! People will begin to sense a stirring inside themselves, but they may not be able to fully verbalize what is happening to them. There is a groaning in people's spirits awaiting the time when God will implement His Kingdom on the earth. That is why yielding to the Spirit of God is essential to our victories in prayer.

> *People know when things are about to happen.*
> *They have a stirring, even an urgency, inside.*

Sons of God

The apostle Paul told all believers in the Book of Romans:

> *For I consider that the sufferings of this present time are not worthy to be compared with the glory which shall be revealed in us. For the earnest expectation of the* ***creation eagerly waits for the revealing of the sons of God*** (Romans 8:18-19).

This is profound. We do not see ourselves the way we should. However, even creation knows who we are and that we exist. I pray right now that the Holy Spirit would reveal who you are in Him. This is our destiny and will cause us to pray with urgency for revelation.

> *Beloved, now we are* ***children of God****; and it has not yet been revealed what we shall be, but we know that when He is revealed, we shall be like Him, for we shall see Him as He is. And everyone who has this hope in Him purifies himself, just as He is pure* (1 John 3:2-3).

> *But those who are counted worthy to attain that age, and the resurrection from the dead, neither marry nor are given in marriage; nor can they die anymore, for they are equal to the angels and are* ***sons of God, being sons of the resurrection*** (Luke 20:35-36).

Favor! I hear this all the time from the Lord: "If you hadn't done this for Me, Kevin, this particular supernatural provision would not have happened for you. Thank you for obeying Me!"

ABOUT DR. KEVIN ZADAI

Kevin Zadai, ThD, was called to ministry at the age of ten. He attended Central Bible College in Springfield, Missouri, where he received a Bachelor of Arts in theology. Later, he received training in missions at Rhema Bible College. He is currently ordained through Rev. Dr. Jesse and Rev. Dr. Cathy Duplantis. At age thirty-one, during a routine day surgery, he found himself on the "other side of the veil" with Jesus. For forty-five minutes, the Master revealed spiritual truths before returning him to his body and assigning him to a supernatural ministry. Kevin holds a commercial pilot license and is retired from Southwest Airlines after twenty-nine years as a flight attendant. He and his lovely wife, Kathi, reside in New Orleans, Louisiana.

OTHER BOOKS BY DR. KEVIN ZADAI

Heavenly Visitation

Heavenly Visitation Study Guide

Heavenly Visitation Prayer Guide

Days of Heaven on Earth

Days of Heaven on Earth Study Guide

Days of Heaven on Earth Prayer Guide

A Meeting Place with God

Your Hidden Destiny Revealed

Salvation Prayer

Lord God,

I confess that I am a sinner. I confess that I need Your Son, Jesus. Please forgive me in His name.

Lord Jesus, I believe You died for me and that You are alive and listening to me now.

I now turn from my sins and welcome You into my heart. Come and take control of my life. Make me the kind of person You want me to be.

Now, fill me with Your Holy Spirit who will show me how to live for You. I acknowledge You before men as my Savior and my Lord.

In Jesus's name.

Amen.

If you prayed this prayer, please contact us at:
info@warriornotes.com for more information and material.
Go to warriornotes.com for other exciting ministry materials.
Warriornotes.com